I read this book ⟨...⟩ was first publis⟨...⟩ continuous stimu⟨...⟩ day to seek and ⟨...⟩ revival and for God's presence among ⟨...⟩ people.

Roger Forster

Nothing is more needed today than the powerful presence of God active in the people of God. Here is a story of expectant people visited by God in revival power. It has much to teach us about the importance of handling such holy things with care, weighing all things by the standard of Scripture, while being prepared unconditionally for God the Holy Spirit to deal with us as He wills. May this eyewitness account of revival awaken that deep desire for His coming that will prepare us for another awakening in our day!

R T Kendall

What an extraordinary book! Real encouragement and inspiration from those at the heart of a great move of God. This important book sheds clear light on recent events, and has a wonderful message for the new millennium.

Dr Patrick Dixon, author of *Signs of Revival*

Christian Focus Publications publishes biblically-accurate books for adults and children. The books in the adult range are published in three imprints.

Christian Heritage contains classic writings from the past.

Christian Focus contains popular works including biographies, commentaries, doctrine, and Christian living.

Mentor focuses on books written at a level suitable for Bible College and seminary students, pastors, and others; the imprint includes commentaries, doctrinal studies, examination of current issues, and church history.

For a free catalogue of all our titles, please write to
Christian Focus Publications,
Geanies House, Fearn,
Ross-shire, IV20 1TW, Great Britain

For details of our titles visit us on our web site
http://www.christianfocus.com

THIS IS THAT

The Spirit of Revival

A first-hand account of the Congo Revival of the 1950s

"But **this is that** which was spoken by the prophet
Joel; and it shall come to pass in the last days, saith
God, I will pour out of my Spirit upon all flesh...."
Acts 2:16,17

Christian Focus
WEC

© WEC International
ISBN 185792 611 0
First published in 1954 by Christian Literature Crusade
Reissued with new Introduction 2000

Published by
Christian Focus Publications, Geanies House, Fearn,
Ross-shire, IV20 1TW, Great Britain
and by
WEC International, Bulstrode, Oxford Road,
Gerrards Cross, Bucks, SL9 8SZ, Great Britain.

Cover design by Owen Daily

Contents

INTRODUCTION

As I read a letter asking me if I would consider writing an introduction for a re-issue of 'This is That', my heart raced – memories flooded back.

That last Friday evening in July 1953 – I remember it as though it were yesterday! It was 7.00pm: one hundred of us gathered for the weekly fellowship meeting in the Bible School hall at Ibambi, in the north-eastern province of what was then the Belgian Congo, later Zaire, now again the Democratic Republic of Congo. Jack Scholes, leader of the team of 50 missionaries working across the province, had stood to lead in prayer. We had sung a hymn, and Jack began to share what he had witnessed of revival in the southern part of the mission area, where he had been visiting during the previous two weeks.

Suddenly, all heard the fearful roar of an approaching hurricane. Stewards moved round the hall, taking down the wooden shutters to prevent accidents that could occur, should they be blown in.

I glanced out into the night, expecting to see dark scudding clouds, palm trees bending low to the ground, dust spirals rushing towards us – it simply wasn't there! The clear sky, upright palm trees silhouetted in the moonlight, all was still, utterly still. Yet the storm lanterns, suspended from the central beam the length of the hall, were shaking wildly! The very building seemed to rock, as though a rumbling earthquake was beginning to erupt. A noise as of a rushing mighty wind filled the place.

All over the hall, people were down on the ground, crying out to God for mercy. Others were shaking violently, apparently uncontrollably. Here and there, a few were on their feet, their hands upraised, their faces radiant, praising God.

What on earth was happening? Was this the work of the Holy Spirit, visiting us in revival blessing, or was it a demonic spirit seeking to disrupt the fellowship? Was it for real, or was it a great deception?

Jack Scholes stood still, watching, praying, and then moving forward amongst us, speaking quietly to one and another of the leading elders, pastors and missionaries: 'Just pray! Ask God to keep control: allow the Holy Spirit freedom to act as He sees fit.'

All over the hall, a shattering conviction of sin was gripping hearts. Sin was suddenly seen as desperately sinful. There were no gradations, big or small – sin was sin, and separated one from God. People were moved to tears, and almost forced by the Spirit of God to confess – to confess to petty thieving, jealousies, anger, coldness of heart, spiritual pretence.... And then, as sin was brought out and laid at the foot of the Cross, cleansed by the precious blood of the Saviour, an amazing joy flooded in! Singing started – in great waves – words being made up as they sang, each song praising God for the Blood.

"Fura'a, Fura'a, Fura'a, Kwa damu ya Yesu!"

"Joy, Joy, Joy For the blood of Jesus!"

The 7.00 pm evening meeting would always be finished by 9.00 pm – many of us were still there at 2.00 am! Some stayed all night. And all through Saturday. And Saturday night. By Sunday, the news had spread of the Spirit's gracious visitation to the 'big church' at Ibambi, and Christians began arriving from the surrounding villages. Throughout the day, the Holy Spirit continued His wonderful work. Many were broken down under conviction of sin, then led into a new realisation of cleansing and forgiveness. By afternoon, joy – joy of an extraordinary power and wonder – filled the vast crowd. The singing, the radiant faces, arms upraised at every mention of the Name of Jesus – what a day!

And the revival swept on, village by village, over the whole region, through the ensuing months, the ensuing years. The church doubled its numbers – and then trebled. Twelve years later, when civil war tore our country apart, the revived church had been prepared by God to withstand the onslaught of unbelievable horror and evil.

As you read the following chapters, written nearly fifty years ago by eye-witnesses in the full flush of the fires of revival blessing, do not be put off by language or vocabulary that was acceptable then, even though no longer so now. To be a 'houseboy' was considered a privilege! It was not 'colonial' to employ a local person to help in the home or kitchen; in fact, it was demanded by the Government, as a condition of one's right to live there, that foreigners employed local people. The title 'native' was not then derogatory or paternalistic: it simply referred to the people born in the country – today known as nationals.

The fact that the revival is mainly reported as God working in the hearts and lives of African nationals does not mean that He was not equally working in the missionaries – just that there was only one pale-skinned foreigner to every ten thousand dark-skinned nationals! And the prevailing interest was in what God was doing in the midst of our Africans, not really in what He was also doing among the missionaries.

I can never thank God enough for His gracious patience with me. For four years, I resisted the convicting work of the Spirit, too proud to break and publicly confess to spiritual dryness and failure. But He did not let me go! In 1957, through the prayers of revived Africans, and the ministry of my African Pastor, Ndugu, I too was released from the bondage of my pride, and brought, by God's gracious Spirit, into the full flow of the blessing – through confession of sins, cleansing by the Blood, infilling with joy, and an overwhelming realisation of a new power for witness and for teaching the Word.

Dear Pastor Ndugu died at the close of 1999, probably about one hundred years old. He never lost the joy of his salvation. The work of God in his heart and life were clearly evident to the end of his long life. But the experience of those amazing weeks and months in 1953 had brought him into an even fuller experience of God's love and grace, and most particularly into a deep understanding of God's word. He had become a dynamic preacher of Biblical truth, as well as a tender-hearted pastor in the care of his flock.

There are others like him, who to this day, have never looked back in their Christian walk, since their baptism in the Holy Spirit in those amazing days of revival.

May we, as we re-read this account of an outpouring of the Spirit on the Church in Congo, allow the Spirit to stir our hearts afresh and to challenge us deeply as to the reality of our own spiritual experience today. May we not quibble over language (references to the Holy Ghost, rather than the Spirit; to lepers, rather than to men and women suffering from the disease of leprosy; and other such terms), but rather be constrained to seek a fresh anointing on our own lives, with an equipping power for the ministry to which God calls each one of us in these days of unparalleled opportunity for witness and service.

Helen Roseveare
January 2000

FOREWORD

THE area in which there has been this recent mighty outpouring of the Spirit, of which these pages tell, is the exact centre of the continent of Africa, in the North-east Belgian Congo. It was the field first entered in 1914 by C. T. Studd and A. B. Buxton, who founded there what was originally called The Heart of Africa Mission, and which later developed into the larger society, The Worldwide Evangelization Crusade.

From 1914 onwards an area of some 400 miles long and 250 broad at its widest part has been gradually occupied, a gospel witness being established among numerous tribes, with a staff averaging fifty missionaries in ten centres. For some years now there has been an indigenous African Church spread over this area, numbering many thousands, and worshipping in several hundred village churches under the leadership of their own village elders, each of whom can read and in some measure expound the Scriptures. Trained evangelists, who have been to the Central Bible School, are located at some of the larger churches with a ministry extending into the district around them. A few who are called

'Pastors' – elected by the churches – men of spiritual maturity, have an itinerant ministry of edification in the various areas.

It is among this church of Christ in the heart of Africa that the Spirit has now come in such astounding revival power, reminiscent of the days of the Acts of the Apostles. As it has been so manifestly a work of God Himself, so largely transmitted from place to place through the witness of the revived Africans, the missionaries felt that all glory would go to God if none of their names were mentioned in the letters quoted. Most of the letters are from the missionaries in charge of the various centres, who have been in the work anything from fifteen to over thirty years, earnestly waiting and watching for God to visit His people in power. With what joy they have co-operated in His mighty workings, and report on them as those who can take a mature and balanced view of what is happening. Occasionally names of Africans are mentioned, as they will mean nothing to most readers. Quoting mainly from the letters of the missionaries in charge means that they naturally speak largely of what they have seen themselves; but they wish it to be understood that all the missionary staff in the various centres have been teams together in the Spirit in this ministry.

Much will be learned, by those keen to learn, from the variety of experiences and observations of the missionaries, of the ways of the Spirit and the use of the Word in such a day of visitation; but above all, of the absolute necessity of the Lord suddenly coming to His temple and 'sitting as a refiner and purifier of silver' in every part of His church on earth, if the false is to be separated from the true, and if the true are to shine as lights in the world, holding forth the Word of life.

May these testimonies leave their indelible mark on any of us who are looking for a church in our generation, revived, 'terrible as an army with banners', a resurrected agent of a resurrected Christ.

The General Secretary
The Worldwide Evangelization Crusade
August 1954.

I

THE BEGINNING

THE first news, without any previous warning, reached us in a letter from the missionary in charge of Lubutu, dated February 9 1953. Lubutu is an eighteen-year-old mission centre at the southern extremity of our field, deep in the forest, where there are now small congregations of believers in numerous surrounding villages.

"We share this good news with you," he wrote. "This past week we have been holding our workers' conference, and all our African evangelists are with us, some seventy odd, including wives. We had prepared messages on the Holy Spirit, each speaker dealing with one particular aspect. After the first message the Africans expressed among themselves a desire for God to meet with them. The church business lasted all that day without anything startling happening. In the evening, however, we Europeans were holding our usual prayer meeting in our house, while the Africans were meeting for theirs in the school. Suddenly we heard strange loud cryings coming from the

17

building. Going along to see, we found people shaking all over the place. Many were quite overcome with a violent shaking, quite uncontrollable. After a time we sought to close the meeting, but it went on for hours. Many were standing with their hands raised, worshipping the Saviour. Some were bringing out hidden secrets, confessing them not to us, but to some unseen Person. My colleague was awakened about midnight by his boy, still shaking, coming to confess pilfering things in his house. And so it went on.

"We hardly knew what to say. We had been praying for a long time for revival, but were not expecting anything of this kind, and wondered if it were a spurious movement. Praise God, we found it to be a touch of revival. The evangelists had met together for prayer and to discuss the possibility of receiving a new anointing of the Holy Spirit. Some who held grievances one against the other got right. Then they arrived at the point of asking, 'What shall we do now? Let us go and ask the missionaries to lay hands on us.' They had read this for themselves in the New Testament. Others had doubts about this, and while they puzzled it out, the Holy Ghost Himself fell upon them. Many said they felt their hearts just burn with joy. It would appear that the spiritual experience was so great that many were quite overcome. Not all had this overpowering experience, but all had the joy of the Lord. To use their own expression, 'The Holy Spirit came as the dew, none was left out.' Our own hearts have been stirred and revived, and we are expecting this revival to spread. Instead of heaviness, our people are now on the leash to get out in the district to preach and testify. They are not going away with a new determination this time, but with a new power. It was wonderful to hear the testimonies on Sunday afternoon. The Lord has suddenly come to His temple, in this case the African Church."

2

A TORNADO OF BLESSING

SOME months later, while we were still hearing news of the Lord's working at Lubutu, letters began to reach us from our next centre, Opienge, to the north, telling of the mighty workings of the Spirit among them. The missionary in charge sent us the story in full details.

"I had told the natives of the Ruanda blessing," he wrote, "and also of that in Korea, so that much prayer had gone up for a work of the Holy Spirit, although they were not fully aware what form such a work would actually take, but there were longings for something deeper in their own hearts, and to see souls saved. There were one or two signs of the Lord wanting to do a new thing among us, but we were slow to recognize them. One was the experience which one of our evangelists went through when he had had some words with his wife. He took up a twig and struck her once on the arm. Immediately he was overcome by a terrible outburst of remorse, and had to be forcibly carried into another house, where he continued all night crying out to the Lord to wipe away his sin. We now recognize the tremblings that came upon him as the same as have been experienced by many since. Another sign was the spirit of conviction that came upon six of our elders during some special meetings some months before 'the tornado of blessing' broke upon us in May. But we did not recognize the signs, because we were expecting the Lord to work in revival according to a certain preconceived plan.

"We had heard of the move of the Spirit at Lubutu, and although we praised the Lord for the visitation, we were not impressed by the account of the manifestations. We began to fear what the Government would say, and would the thing get out of hand. The natives, however, were very interested, and prayed that they, too, would thus be blessed. A few of the women then began to come to my wife, concerned about their coldness, and we too were concerned at the materialism and lack of concern for the lost. Everyone seemed bent on getting more of this world's goods than the other fellow. I think the women realized their failings, but had no power to be different. We wondered if our work was finished here. We seemed to be tired in our spirits with a losing battle, yet outwardly the work was going on fine and the Church being added to daily.

"The next move was when Sena, the wife of a Lubutu elder, came up to Opienge on a visit. My co-worker and I were on trek at the time. She came to the Sunday service, and people noticed jerks and shakings of her body during the meetings. One or two approached her, thinking that she was ill. She told them she was not ill, but that the Holy Spirit was upon her. People were amazed, and not a few amused. Nothing else happened until the Tuesday night, when Peleza, the wife of the Opienge chief elder, woke up other folk with her loud singing and praises. They flocked to her house and saw her on the bed in an upright position shaking violently and saying, 'Thanks, thanks, thanks, Lord Jesus', over and over again. They thought she had gone mad. As she got quieter, they went back to their houses, but at 4.00 a.m. she again woke them up singing, 'There is light in my heart'. She told them she had seen a light come closer and closer to her, until it eventually burst upon her and filled her heart. Folk were amazed, some laughed and said, 'She is gone off top', but others rebuked them, saying it was better to wait and see if it was the Lord's doing. It was then she got a vision from the Lord. She saw a great light, and a voice said to her, 'Peleza, I want to do a great work here at Opienge, but there is much hardness. If you want to light a good fire, do you get one by laying the wood among the ashes?' 'No,' she answered. Then the voice asked, 'What must be done then?' 'Clean away the ashes first.' 'That is right,' the voice said, 'I want a clean place for my fire.' The following Sunday the Spirit again came upon Peleza in the service, and although she was asked to be still, the shakings were beyond her control.

"As I said, we were out on trek when a letter reached us, telling us of these happenings. After I had read it, I got a vision from the Lord of what was going to happen. I saw the meetings with the people shouting, shaking, and making confession – all the manifestations which we have now seen. The vision shook me, and I got a fear of the whole thing. My own inability brought a fear, as I knew the people would crowd to me for help, and a great longing came to run away from it all; but I prayed to the Lord to help me, and came through willing to be used. It is one thing to pray for revival, quite another to be willing for it.

"Before returning to the station, I had another vision. A hard rock was standing up before me. I saw blood running over the face of it, and while I watched, the blood congealed. I wondered at the vision, but did not understand it. When I got back, the thought came to me strongly to look up the meaning of the word 'congeal', and I found, 'Congealed is the state some liquids become when poured over a cold surface.' Then I understood. It was the same message as Peleza had had.

"Peleza came to tell me of her experience and of the rumours that were being spread about her. The week passed off quietly until the Thursday, which was our monthly day of prayer. Peleza then came asking that the men and women divide into separate meetings, as she wished to testify to the women alone. The meeting with the women, at which some began to confess sins, went on till mid-morning. At the second meeting with the men, after I had urged them to be open to the Spirit, we turned to prayer. We had hardly started when we noticed a different note in the prayer of the evangelist who had struck his wife, a great pleading note, an earnestness which tended to be extreme. He seemed very agitated, and was soon crying, tears flowing freely. He ended by falling down on the seat. There was a silence for a few moments, then the chief elder, a very tall man, shot up to his full height, his hands stretched out, shaking and shouting at the top of his voice, 'Thanks, thanks, Lord Jesus.' In no time the whole place was as if charged with an electric current. Men were falling, jumping, laughing, crying, singing, confessing, and some shaking terribly. It was a terrible sight. One man came upon his hands and knees from the back of the room right up to the front. A young man had a mighty filling. His shakings and jumpings were awful to behold, then he turned to praise and came out to a large place, praise ascending to the Throne such as I had never heard before from an African. He had nothing to confess, as he was already in a healthy place with the Lord.

"During this time the women had come out of their meeting and had gathered round the windows to see the wonderful spectacle of their men being so possessed, then instead of going back to their homes to prepare food, they turned and went back to their meeting-place. Hardly had they got there, when the Spirit came down upon them, and the same manifestations were seen among them. Even when both meetings had finished, folks were falling down praising the Lord, or confessing their sins on the paths or in the village. The afternoon meeting was united, and what a meeting! I had been reading *Rent Heavens*, by R. B. Jones, on the Welsh revival, and in it he mentioned that 'the evangelist could hardly make his voice heard above the din of the worshipping saints'. How true that has been of the meetings we have seen out here. This particular one can best be described as a spiritual tornado. People were literally flung to the floor or over the forms, yet no one was hurt. It was here I was first led to challenge an excess of emotionalism, for one or two women who were flung to the floor did not take heed to their clothes, so I rebuked them, and later spoke of the Holy Spirit being a holy Spirit in the true sense of the word. The people responded well. Time after time they were willing to be taught, and accepted almost without question any exhortation backed by the Word. The girls from the school were present, and the Lord began a mighty work among them. The schoolboys, except for two or three, were not touched.

"That evening we missionaries got together for prayer. None of us had ever seen anything like this before. I had been in many wonderful prayer meetings at the Bible College of Wales, Swansea, when the Spirit had come down upon us in power, but nothing like this. So I asked the Lord to give us the spirit of discernment, and I believe He did. I praise the Lord also for the unity He gave, for many questions came up such as, 'Is this of the Lord or not?' But as we went on together holding on to the Lord, He gave us all the assurance that 'This is that' of Acts 2:16.

"Next day, Friday, was a day of humbling to us missionaries. We had to hear confession after confession of the things the people had held against us, as they came to ask for forgiveness for murmuring and grumbling against us. It was then that I was first led to test the Spirit and prove the blessing. I must confess that even up to that time there were still questionings in my heart. So I challenged those who had confessed to stealing to make restitution, and I praise the Lord that there was a ready response. During the next week I put the following tests:

(1) Is there a love for the truth, and are you sensitive to it?

(2) What is your attitude to a lie? Is it hateful to you?

(3) Are you willing, as far as possible, to put a wrong right by making restitution or asking forgiveness of the person wronged?

(4) Are you willing to make a public confession of the Lord Jesus?

(5) Does the praise go to the Lord?

These tests have been fully met over and over again. People have gone long distances to clear up misunderstandings. Folk have cried as if breaking their hearts because they had misrepresented something, and pleaded for forgiveness. When challenged to make restitution, some have dashed off to fetch money to pay back a bad debt. Our boy was a case in point. When the Spirit came upon him, he got up and made a full confession of all the things he had stolen from us, and brought back money to pay for them. He had also stolen kerosene from a trader, but was afraid to repay for fear of prison; but when challenged by the Spirit through a message on Zacchaeus he went and made it right. The same trader has been amazed at the number of people who have come to confess stealing. As for testimony and praise, there has not been time enough for all who wanted to testify, and there has never been such praise to the Lord in these parts. Mr. Rees Howells used to speak of 'savage joy', and it has been true in some of our meetings. I hardly thought that Kingwana lent itself to the expression of such praise, but the Holy Spirit causes these souls to praise the Lord Jesus from hearts full of joy, a beautiful thing to behold. 'Out of the mouth of babes and sucklings thou hast perfected praise' has been fulfilled here.

"The following Saturday the people from the villages began to arrive for the week of special meetings arranged long before, some walking nearly 100 miles to attend. 'What will happen in the coming week?' was the question on many lips. That evening there were about

28

400 people crowded into the building, and I gave a welcome message, urging them to be ready for the Lord and telling what had happened on the previous Thursday. Then, as I led in prayer, the Spirit came down in mighty power, sweeping through the congregation. My whole body trembled with the power. We then saw a marvellous sight, people literally filled and drunk with the Spirit. Never have we seen anything like this. The power and presence of the Lord were awful indeed. Elders and evangelists were swept to their feet, reeling around like drunken men, shouting out, 'I am filled! I am filled!' Then some of them turned to me and asked for forgiveness for having criticized me. As soon as I said I had forgiven them, they praised the Lord in mighty and loud praises. They went to one another, or called out a name at the other end of the building, asking for forgiveness for some wrong done. Another called out the name of his wife, telling her he was filled with the Spirit and urging her not to hold out against the Lord. One evangelist made public confession that he had made wrong entries in his report book.

"There was unbounded joy in the meeting. One elder was clapping his hands and thighs in an ecstasy of joy, yet at the same time failing to stand upright and staggering like a man drunk, his knees refusing to function properly. Elder Leon became like a lion, marching up and down the aisle, praising the Lord with mighty shouts, then turning first to the men, then to the women, next to the schoolgirls and boys, urging them to turn to the Lord, saying that He was soon returning. Men, women, boys, and girls were overcome by the power of the Spirit. It was impossible to make out what folk were saying. Some were praising, some were in an agony of soul, crying with copious tears rolling down their faces, unashamed. Others were dancing and jumping before the Lord through sheer joy, others shaking uncontrollably and shouting out, 'Praise the Lord!' over and over again. Others were singing away on their own, quite unconscious of what the rest were doing.

"I felt led to clap my hands and start the hymn 'Onward Christian Soldiers'. Immediately, like one man, the whole congregation was on its feet, and was there ever singing like it? No, not even in my native Wales, except perhaps during the revival. On the singing went, every line, every verse with punctuated emphasis, people glancing at their neighbours with a smile indicating their fullness of joy at the victory of Jesus. There was such a volume of praise that angels must have stopped their ministering to gaze down at the wonderful sight. The hymn was sung over and over again, until hallelujahs ended a wonderful meeting, and we drifted out of the building about midnight. For many there was no sleep, but singing and praising and souls getting right with God all through the night.

"Next day, Sunday, we had our first test of fanaticism with a young man dashing up early in the morning, very agitated and shouting out that he had a message from the Lord for the Government official. But I was convinced that it was not the Holy Spirit and challenged him. He accused me of hindering the Spirit and dashed off to the Government post; but the official was not there. I called the evangelists and elders together and gave them from the Word the danger of some people giving place to the devil, and urged them to instruct the people to obey those that are over them in the Lord and that watch for their souls (Heb. 13:17). We are thrilled at the way people respond to exhortation from the Word, and so far we have been spared many such affairs. Another case was a man who for years had wanted to be 'some great one', but the elders had to rebuke him time and time again for low living. He came to me early one morning saying that the Spirit had given him a message to visit me behind closed doors and lay his hands on me that I might receive the Spirit. Knowing the man, the Spirit led me to challenge him in the name of Jesus, that he had never received the Holy Spirit. He went away and has not bothered me nor the people any more.

"During the Sunday the spiritual tempo of the meetings grew. It was difficult to deliver a message. We began to realize that the Lord was working in two different ways. At first the people would say of one who was thrown to the ground or was under the influence of the Spirit, that he was filled by the Spirit. But the realization came that this was not so. The mighty filling of the Holy Spirit of those who were ready to receive Him was beautiful to behold, and their joy knew no bounds. But the others, shaking under a terrible conviction of sin, were a different sight altogether. There were many who, after asking for forgiveness, had no joy, and we saw the danger of many believing that they had now got all, and there was nothing else, because they had had an experience of shaking. We showed them the possibility of a clean, garnished house being empty, and the danger of that man's latter state being worse than the first, if he did not claim the filling of the Holy Spirit as in Luke 11:13.

"I felt the need of asking that room be made in the meetings for teaching from the Word. In accounts of the Lord's visitations in other places, it is often said that ministers do not carry on with the preaching and teaching, the meetings being given over to testimony, prayer, and singing, etc. But I found that a continual bringing of the Word to the people has meant that many have seen truths from the Scriptures that went unnoticed before. The quoting of Scripture by the people has also been an outstanding feature of all testimonies as well as utterances in prayer.

"One aspect of the Spirit's working was what we came to call 'the prompters'. When a person is under the influence of the Spirit and in agony through terrible conviction, the Spirit comes on another person who will start prompting the convicted one with such sentences as, 'Bring it all out! Don't hide anything! Jesus is ready to forgive! Think back! There is still more to confess! The big sin still remains!' It is amazing how the convicted ones respond to such promptings, even when many are praying aloud at the same time, and 'the prompter' is away at the back of the building.

"A young man called Tomasi was greatly used in this way, also an old gardener, both of whom are very ordinary folk; yet the persons confessing responded in an amazing way to their promptings.

"Some folk would be in such an agony through the Spirit of conviction upon them, that their cries were pitiful, yet there was nothing we could do, so we urged the people to pray. Those continual urgings to prayer have led them into a wonderful praying attitude which has become a feature of most meetings. As soon as a person gets up to pray, practically the whole congregation will pray simultaneously, some standing, some sitting, without any disorder or confusion.

"On one occasion we saw the enemy trying to lead people astray. It was when some folk were giving their testimonies, and I noticed that, though they were people who had confessed sin the previous night and had a time of praising the Lord for forgiveness, they were now asking Him to forgive them again, instead of testifying to His glory. One or two had already sat down, before the Lord brought this to my notice. I straightway challenged the next and asked if he had not praised for forgiveness the previous night. Yet the next to speak did exactly the same thing. Then I recognized the hand of the enemy in putting unbelief into the hearts of young converts. So I stopped the testimonies and asked the people to pray. What a hard time we had! But after pleading with the Lord to give us victory, we came out into a large place with a great shout of victory in the camp.

"Some folk have criticized us for what they termed 'taking a hand' in the revival, on the ground that the Holy Spirit is well able to deal with the people; but there is a great difference between hindering the Spirit in His work, and being used by the Spirit. I praise the Lord from a full heart that the evangelists and elders were so one with us during those wonderful meetings. Together we learned lessons, and now they are being used in wondrous ways in the area.

"After the folk had returned to their villages, we had a very busy time on the station. Nearly everyone had some affair to put right or debt to settle. One ex-houseboy brought a flowered soup-plate to my wife, saying he wished her to accept it, as when he was with us he had smashed so many of our dishes that the Spirit had convicted him and told him to show his sorrow in this practical way. Our present houseboy handed her some money, saying it was for needles and money he had stolen. At first we were inclined to refuse the money, but the Lord led us to accept, showing us that it was good for their own soul's sake to make proper restitution. Another point in our houseboy's testimony was when he said,

'These white people like their beds made every day. That is one of my jobs. As my white lady was busy with her duties of school and medicine, I hardly ever did my job thoroughly; but now since the Holy Spirit has come into my life, that bed gets done every day!' Others even among the leaders of the Church have confessed to unfaithfulness, and have been willing, when the Church thought fit, to be disciplined. One of the elders had seen many of his friends being blessed, but himself had had no such experience. I happened to be looking in his direction in one meeting and saw him glancing round at this and that one actively filled with the Spirit. Then I saw him trying to 'work up' the blessing by shaking and trembling all over. After a few minutes of this, he gave it up and was looking very sorry for himself for the rest of the evening. A few weeks later, my co-worker heard him testify, after he had experienced the real thing, to his attempt to 'work up' the blessing, and his failure. His case, and that of one or two others, gave us the opportunity of pointing out the danger of counterfeit.

"The people were amazed at the sensitiveness of the Holy Spirit to what they called small sins. The breaking of the sixth, seventh, and eighth commandments they understood, but heart sins like murmuring, evil thoughts, and criticism they had thought He would not be so particular about. But when they came under terrible conviction over such sins, then they saw them as God sees them. Tunziako, for instance, had spoken a lot against a certain missionary. For days the Spirit strove with her. She would tremble terribly and get up to confess a certain wrong, but still there would be no freedom or joy. Later she would tremble again and cry piteously, asking that a certain hymn be sung, but still no freedom, until one day I was asked to go and see her, as she couldn't walk. My colleague and I went. She was sitting on a low stool and couldn't move her legs. I tried to help her rise, but it was impossible, her legs seemed fixed or stuck to the ground. We sat down near her, and all the time she was crying pitifully. Then she began to bring out with great sorrow of heart her sin of speaking against the missionary. As soon as she had finished, she was filled with joy, her knees straightened, and she stood and walked. There have been other cases of limbs fixed. One who never comes to any meetings was on his way to his wine palm to drink, when he was arrested by a deep conviction of sin. Both his hands came together at the wrists with a sense of heat, and he could not part them.

Then his legs came together in the same manner, and he fell into a sitting position on the road. He then confessed his sins. The Spirit then told him, 'I will release your legs so that you can walk back to your village and tell the folk, but your hands will remain fixed until you have obeyed.' He did so, much to the astonishment of his wife and others, and as soon as he had obeyed his hands were released. An elder went out to visit him and teach him more fully the way of the Lord. He and his wife then accepted the Saviour.

"At one of the meetings, while listening to some folk confessing to the Lord, I looked toward the window, and there was a woman named Mada whom I knew lived in sin. The Spirit bade me raise my hand and point to her and ask her when she was coming to the Lord. A few days later, when our boy was testifying in the village, Mada was listening and was suddenly thrown violently to the ground, trembling all over and crying out to the Lord for forgiveness. Next Sunday she testified in the meetings to having been born again. And so the story goes on. Such testimonies could be added to by the score, and we praise the Lord that there is every evidence of the blessing going deep in the lives of many. Some seem to have grown up spiritually in a night, as it were.

"We were led to call a prayer meeting three evenings a week, in addition to any other meetings held. They have been a mighty power house. What prayer! They were not selfish prayers, as we were led to pray that the blessing would spread to the other stations. What shouts of praise go forth as word has come to us week by week of one station after another being reached by the spirit of revival.

"A phenomenon, which we whites have not yet seen, but which some of our best evangelists and Christians vouch for, is that of seeing a holy light in some of their houses. Many people have seen it in the girls' dormitory on more than one occasion, here on the mission station (Acts 12:7).

"Visions have been given to some of the people, many on the second coming. One of our best women described how she had seen the rapture, the Lord coming in the clouds, and hearing the trump of God, and seeing the shining ones and lots of people on earth looking up, and folks' feet leaving the ground and gently ascending to meet the Lord; then seeing the folks left behind, some spreading their arms and trying to rise, but unable to do so, and the look of horror on their faces. Folks that heard her describe it were very moved. One evangelist had a remarkable vision. He saw a wheel revolving in the air and was told that that endless revolving represented the prayers of those who prayed formally. Then the vision changed and he saw a great column of smoke ascending and forming a vast cloud, which in turn appeared as if it were driven earthwards. He was told that the cloud represented the prayers of the Spirit-filled believers formed into a mighty weapon in God's hands to be used for the good of the nations, meaning revival. The recounting of this vision has been a blessing to many to pray without ceasing.

"The spreading of the blessing to the district around has been most encouraging in some areas. We hear also of Roman Catholic native teachers who are left all alone, since their flock has accepted the Lord and no more believe in their rituals.

"The attitude of some government officials can be seen from the words of a nearby Administrator to some witchcraft people with whom he was dealing: 'Why do you stick to this false religion? Look at what is happening at the missionaries' place. Where did the blessing come from? The ground? The forest? No, it came from heaven, it is the real thing. They are praying for us whites, and we need it. So do you. Leave your witchcraft and go there for the real things.' "

3

A MISSIONARY IS PREPARED

A visit of two of the missionaries from Opienge, with some Africans, to the Bomili area, was the means of the revival reaching them. Bomili, in the section of the Ituri forest occupied by the Babari tribe, has had a mission centre for a number of years, but recently a fresh start was made on a new site. The building was filled with 800 people for the first meeting, and after two messages the Spirit came down in mighty power on the whole congregation with similar manifestations to Opienge. Here, too, there had been preparations of heart, especially in the case of one out-church leader in training, with whom God dealt some weeks before with shakings and confession of secret sin, and then with a heavy burden for the lost; though working during the day at brick-making, he spent whole nights in prayer and praise, going to work on the following days with a testimony that he was as fresh as if he had slept the night through. The power fell upon the packed building, with others standing around the windows, while an African woman from Opienge was giving her testimony. It was as bewildering and overwhelming as in the other centres, amongst adults, boys and girls. In this instance one of the lady missionaries at Bomili tells of her own special preparation of heart for the coming blessing:

"Throughout the school term I had been burdened for the girls that they might be truly born again. I had spoken much on true salvation, not only of repenting of their sin, necessary as that is, but also of receiving Christ into their hearts by faith, as many don't seem to receive a positive experience when they repent. How I longed that the message should find a resting place in their hearts, and that they might understand and receive Jesus as their life. One night, burdened for their souls and praying for enduement from on high, and whilst rededicating myself to His service, a strange sensation came over me, my heart was pounding, prayer was pouring out of me, and my body began to tremble. I was afraid, for I felt that I was probably allowing my emotions to overcome me, and I tried to still this strange experience.

"From that day I found the messages to the girls charged with new power, power from on high. However short the message was, I felt God was working. He had answered prayer and given power. A week later, while we were having a short season of prayer, as the service closed, the same strange experience came over me and my body began trembling violently. Again afraid of the results, I brought the meeting to an abrupt close. Three days later, while having a prayer meeting with the station women, the Spirit came upon one of the women in a similar way, and a few days previously this woman's husband had leaped from his seat in a prayer meeting, shouting and trembling as the Spirit of God came upon him. A few weeks later we began our week-end conference when close on a thousand people gathered with us from our district churches. We had as our guest speakers the two missionaries from Opienge, and the Africans who accompanied them. God came down in our midst in a wonderful way, and the fire fell. My schoolgirls were leaving to go on holiday the day the conference was to close. I arranged to have a farewell meeting with them. Many confessed to sin of one form or another, such as little unrighteous acts, which had meant nothing to them until the Spirit of God had convicted them. We had a further time of prayer, but I felt a hardness come over the meeting. As I was fervently and silently praying for my girls, this strange sensation I have mentioned came on me again, but now recognizing it for what it was, I did not resist: it seemed that Another Being had taken possession of me, as indeed was true; the Holy Ghost had come, surging through my whole body and reaching even to my finger-tips. In my hands and fingers were sensations like being in contact with live wires: the strangest sensation I have ever experienced, and such as I can never forget. My heart and my whole being were praising God, and as I could keep silent no longer, I let out joyful bursts of hallelujah, which were echoed by my amazed schoolchildren. A few moments later an evangelist's wife came along saying she wanted to pray with the girls. She had heard our shouts and had come to see if she could help. I knew she was sent by God, for He had much more work to do in their hearts, and so I left them in her care. Soon the compound was ringing with their cries, as the Spirit came down in convicting power and confessions of deep sin were made. This went on until about midnight. Yes, revival has come!"

4

OVERWHELMING FLOODS

FROM Lubutu the blessing next spread to our largest centre, Wamba, some seventy miles to the north. For years this has been the most flourishing work on our field, with many outchurches, a strong body of evangelists, and large numbers of boys and girls, both in the bush and station schools. The missionary in charge, writing in October 1953, three months after the Spirit began to move among them, has given us a full account of their experiences. He starts by quoting John 16: 8: "And when He is come, he will reprove the world of sin, and of righteousness and of judgment."

"Ever since Sunday, July 19," he continues, "we have been witnessing, day by day, the truth of these wonderful words. At the very beginning we want to be careful to say that the Doer of the wonderful works we have been seeing is the Holy Spirit spoken of in this text. The conversions have been marvellous: the whole compound is a new place: from missionaries, to workmen and their wives, to school-teachers and their wives, to houseboys, schoolboys, and schoolgirls. We can say Amen to the words of the late Bishop Ryle, 'If it were only a little mending, a little patching, a little turning over of a new leaf, then man might do this. But when it is a translation, a creation, a resurrection, God must do it.'

"The first manifestations of the outpouring of the Holy Spirit began with the return to Wamba of an evangelist and his wife who had spent two years in the Lubutu area. They had seen the start of the revival there, and told the people here of what they had witnessed.

"On Sunday, July 19, the morning service was taken by this evangelist and his wife. There was nothing unusual, apart from the wife's shakings and shouts of 'Hallelujah! Lord Jesus' during the singing. She had been doing this ever since they returned. At the close I gave the usual invitation. When most of the people had left the building, one young schoolteacher turned back and came to sit on the front form. He looked a bit frightened and began to tremble. A girl with paralysed legs sat on the front form of the women's side. We took no notice of her, as she normally sat on until folk had dispersed. But no sooner had Yoane, the teacher, began to speak than the girl, Biboko, began to cry. Her cry rose to a wail, then to a loud howl. I do not know what else to call it.

Oh, the agony of it! She covered her face with her hands, but the tears came flowing through her fingers. When she finally became able to articulate, she cried, 'What shall I do? What shall I do?' a hundred times over. By this time the whole congregation had returned to the meeting. Biboko was crying her heart out, and Yoane was confessing his sins. Another woman, the wife of an elder who had been dismissed for sin, began to tremble, and then to shake violently. Her shakings were quite uncontrollable. At that moment a man came to tell me that my wife wanted me at the house. I hastened over and found a crowd round the door. As I broke through, I saw her bending over a man lying on the floor. He was our head workman. She had found him standing in the room with his arms uplifted, crying in an agony, 'Oh, my heart is wicked, my heart is wicked! Oh, my sins, my sins!' Then he fell headlong to the floor. He lay on his back, shaking and crying to God for mercy. I found her telling him, 'Hide nothing. Confess everything you know. You cannot obtain mercy until you bring everything out', and quoting 1 John 1: 9 to him. What a confession, and what sin! Poor Froma, what it must have cost him to bring out all that hidden sin!

"We asked him if he believed God had

forgiven him on the strength of the promise. He said he did believe. So I took him back to the building and told him to testify to the people. He was still shaking, so we sat him on a chair. With arm uplifted he told the people his sins, and how he now believed God had accepted him in the Lord Jesus. Yoane then testified, so did Biboko, and the other woman. Yoane said he had begun to leave the building with his friends. He had walked but five steps when his legs stiffened and he could not go forward. He heard a voice in his heart warning him that if he left the church without getting right with God he would be a lost soul. He stood there fighting it out. Then he confessed to many disobediences, and at the close of his confession was overwhelmed with the joy of forgiveness. He was the first case of 'drunkenness' we saw. He swayed and sang and laughed. Later, he composed many hymns. The people then dispersed, and we knew we had seen the beginnings of a great movement of the Holy Spirit. Spurgeon once prayed, 'Lord, send us a season of glorious disorder.' We were to see just that – but such wonderful order in disorder!

"That evening, just as we had finished our missionaries' prayers, I was called to go to the workmen's quarters, as God was at work there.

What a sight! I shall never forget it. The little building was packed with men – the women were outside – sitting, standing, lying on the floor, or lying in the arms of others, crying, shouting, confessing, agonizing. One of the men, lying helplessly in the arms of another, kept crying, 'My heart is vile, my heart is vile. Oh, what shall I do? Who can give me a clean heart? I cannot appear before God with this wicked heart!' After he had gone on like this for some time, I went up to him and said, 'You will never get relief by saying your heart is bad. Name your sins and know that the Lord forgives each sin that you confess.' Then he laid bare his heart and confessed to deceit, adultery, drunkenness, etc. With what deep earnestness and remorse he confessed! I cannot put it on paper. But as soon as he had done so, he was filled with joy and praise, and then turned to help his friends who were still in distress.

"Pastor Danga was present with the men when I arrived. I don't know what we should have done without him and a couple of evangelists who were with us at this time. He has been a wonderful help all along. We cannot speak too highly of his spirituality, discernment, and knowledge of God's Word; and how he has enjoyed this wonderful time of God's visitation.

49

"Many of the workmen and school-teachers came through that evening. Some of them had been thrown on the floor and had writhed there until they had finished confessing. One of these, when he rose to his feet, said, 'While I was lying on the floor, God gave me a hymn.' He had already, while on the floor, written about four verses and a chorus. He said God was telling him to sing it, but he did not know to what tune. So he began to sing and compose a tune as he went along. We followed him line by line. It was a good tune, and quite acceptable. That was the first of a whole string of hymns and choruses composed by the men, women, and children. This one was all about the blood of the Lord Jesus and the oil of the Spirit.

"While we were singing, others went under conviction and shook, fell, and cried; some shouted out in agony of spirit. The distress of some was really terrible. The shame of having to confess to adultery and hypocrisy was hard to overcome. But not only did they confess to such gross sins; they also brought out insults, spite, calling names, and strings of sins of bickerings, murmurings, and discontent with the work or wages. A phrase which has become common to us all in these days is 'the whip of the Holy Ghost'. The whip did a wonderful work that night, but that was only the beginning of things. Hardly anyone slept all night. Those who were blessed broke into singing from time to time. Others groaned and cried under conviction of sin. There was a lot of crying among the schoolchildren, especially the girls.

"On Monday morning, at the end of the meeting, one of the men remained in his seat under conviction of sin. When he began to confess, he was joined by others. The women left the meeting, but in a little while one returned. She sat on a form and began to weep; then suddenly she gave a loud cry, jumped to her feet, and raced out of the building. With her arms outstretched, she flung herself down on the ground. I went to her and spoke of God's love and forgiveness of all the sins we confess and forsake. In comparison with some, she had no gross sins to confess, and as soon as she had finished, she said, 'Let us pray.' She prayed aloud and then burst into such wonderful, glad praise. Her tremblings and agonies ceased, and she came straight back and gave her testimony before all the men. Then she stopped abruptly and said, 'Let us pray.' She led in prayer and then gave out a hymn. This was all wonderful to us who knew her, being a very small woman and very quiet. Her boldness was striking.

"While this was happening, Maria, the

house-mother of the schoolgirls, came stalking along the girls' compound, shouting in a language which no one could understand, and waving her arms in a very wild manner. She seemed absolutely mad. I took her by the hand and led her into the building. She said God had given her a new language, and that it was French but there was no French about it. I challenged her to answer questions about the Lord Jesus. This she did satisfactorily and maintained that she loved Him supremely. That relieved me. She calmed down, so I allowed her to go; but she recommenced her wild ways, as I will tell you later.

"We continued to deal with the men. Several came through into grand liberty. One of the workmen had a hard time. He began to tremble most violently, until it took four of us to hold him. What a horrible thing sin is! And when seen in the light of judgement and God's holiness, it is not surprising to hear convicted souls crying out 'Woe is me, for I am undone', as Isaiah did. This man would confess a little, then cry out in sheer agony. He tried to get one word out, but simply could not. Each time he tried, the shaking so got hold of him that he could not utter a word. At last he got it out, and oh, how he shouted it at the top of his voice, and repeated it again and again – LUST. Poor man! It brings tears to my eyes at the thought of it. At last he got rid of the whole burden. Then what joy! We have seen again and again that the folk almost automatically burst into wonderful joy as soon as they had brought out the last known sin. But where there is not a full confession the joy is only superficial, and there will be several shakings until the whole is put under the blood. All the men who had been dealt with eventually got through by about midday – from 6.30 a.m.

"That evening I was again called out to the workmen's quarters. I shall never be able to describe all I saw. There was a strong sense of heaven and hell. Some were in ecstasies of joy, jumping about just like wild men. Others were in fear of hell, lying around, groaning and writhing, the nearest thing to 'wailing and gnashing of teeth' I have ever witnessed. Those who were through came rushing up to tell me of their wonderful relief, now that the burden of sin was off their shoulders. Others came asking forgiveness for deceit, hypocrisy, laziness, and disobedience. When most of the folk got through, the whole scene changed into one of hectic joy. I have never seen anything like it. The women stood outside the building; only one or two of them had come through into blessing. The men linked arms, danced, sang, leapt, threw their arms about in sheer delight; some would shout, 'The Holy Ghost has come', others would call out, 'Thank God for the blood of Jesus', and so on.

"From time to time ones and twos would break away to go and get right with someone they had offended. I heard one school-teacher confessing to another that he had a bad heart against him, because the Madame had made more of the other fellow than of himself. This went on till a late hour. Eventually I suggested to Pastor Danga that the men had better rest. He called them to a halt. They obeyed instantly. That is a remarkable thing we have seen all through the revival – a willingness to obey, to accept exhortation, to take reproof. He asked an evangelist to close in prayer. There was dead silence. One could almost feel the deep spirit of awe and worship. Suddenly one of the men shouted, 'We're not fit to stand in the presence of God. Down on your knees, men!' Down they all went. It thrills me still as I write. It was a wonderful sight to see, arms intertwined and foreheads almost touching the ground. As soon as the prayer was finished, we all stood and sang. Such singing! Then we all returned to our houses, not knowing whether we walked on earth or in the air.

"On Tuesday morning the Spirit of God

came down on the girls. It was the same again. There were the cryings and wailings and sobbing out of their sins. We called all the women from my meeting to help, and we did what we could to lead the children through to salvation. Crowds of passers-by came to the windows to see what was happening. After a couple of hours most of the girls had come through to peace, and we were able to return them to their compound. We tried putting them to school, but it was really hopeless: some were too full of joy to come back to earth, and others too burdened about their sins to pay attention to schooling. Cries of agony and songs of praise kept on breaking out all day. I had put the men to work, thinking it would save them going to excesses, but it was not easy for them. However, they produced more work that day than in two days previously.

"In the evening we went across to the boys' compound. What a sight! Boys in groups dealing with their fellows, some lying on the ground, others on their knees, and yet others dancing and singing for sheer joy. The singing broke out periodically through the night. Most of the women came through during the day and evening. By no means were most of the people dealt with by us whites; by far the majority were dealt with by the natives themselves.

"On Wednesday morning there was a knock at my door at five-twenty. A young fellow was standing there who has been with us for years, through the school and in preparation for the Bible School. It was dark and chilly, so I said, 'Step inside and sit on that cushioned chair while I close the door.' He looked at the chair for a moment, then hid his face in his hand and cried, 'No, Bwana, I am not fit to sit in that chair. That chair is clean: I am unclean.' Down he went on the floor, face down, arms stretched forward. Dear fellow, I am sure he would have gone lower if it were possible. Then he sobbed out his confession. His wife got through yesterday in the girls' meeting. She had been called in to help, but came under conviction herself and opened her heart to God. He was well liked by us all. But oh, the hidden sin! What an awful story of deceit he had to tell. He had spent most of the night crying and opening his heart to God. When he had told his wife everything, he said, 'I must go and tell someone else. You are my wife. Talking to you is like talking to my own flesh. I must go and tell Bwana.' She tried to restrain him, saying, 'Let Bwana sleep till the morning.' Time and again she held him back, until he could refrain no longer. He finally confessed everything, and then broke into wonderful joy.

What a changed man he is now.

"The kindergarten was visited this morning. The Holy Spirit came upon the children during their morning prayer. Some of the houseboys and workmen ran to the school and became personal workers on the spot. One of the lady missionaries' houseboys was such a grumbler that he was dubbed 'The Growler'. But 'The Growler' had been so wonderfully transformed that he was among the personal workers.

"What wonderful joy and singing on the compound today. Boys, girls, men, and women. One of the favourite hymns is, 'I once was a prodigal'. It is repeated again and again, and yet again. In the teachers' compound today, between sessions, there has been singing that reminds me of the joy of the Israelites when the ark was brought into the camp, 'so that the earth rang again'. Some of them sat in groups with their New Testaments open; others gathered round their hymn-books. What eagerness there is for the Word of God. How the people listen to the messages. What sheer delight folk had when we read to them Psalm 126: 'Then we were like them that dream; then was our mouth filled with laughter and our tongue with singing. Then said they among the heathen, The Lord hath done great things for them. . . .' All day long the folk have been making restitution. Even the state officials have felt the repercussions of this. We have been amazed at the sensitiveness to apparently small things. Many have remembered small debts of even twenty years' standing.

"On Thursday two men came to say that Jackie, the son of our head pastor, was lying prostrate on our doorstep. He was a bad boy, twice expelled from school. He was living in the native town and proving a real prodigal. When his mother died a few months ago, he vowed he would kill his father; he blamed him for her death. He also sought witchcraft to kill certain of the missionaries and natives. He went into adultery and wine drinking, although he was only a lad. He vowed that he would never again put his foot inside a place of worship. When the blessing came to the schoolboys, he began to get afraid. One of them felt such concern for him that he went to speak to him. Jackie was impudent. On other occasions Jackie struck him hard in the back with a pounding mortar, but the lad shouted back, 'Even though you strike me, I shall not cease to preach to you and pray for you until you get right with God.' Once or twice Jackie came to the compound to see what was happening. His sister had been blessed and spoke to him. But he was insolent. He said, 'You have all been taken with a bad sickness. Why don't you go to the doctor and get cured?' This evening he determined to come and see for himself what was happening at the meeting. During the message he began to tremble. He was angry with himself and tried to stop the shaking. At last he got up and sat alone outside, trying to control himself. 'Nothing will make me confess my sins,' he said to himself. But the Spirit of God came upon him. He suddenly saw a huge, blazing fire before him, and he knew he was on the way to hell. Fear seized him and he fell to the ground. Some of the men went to help him, but he could not open his mouth. They remained with him for a long time, then finally picked him up and carried him like a sack of flour and laid him at our door. When I arrived, he was flat on his face, his hands trembling. He was crying most touchingly, 'What shall I do?' Then he began confessing. It just poured out. Again he would cry, 'Oh, God, forgive me; God have mercy on me; what shall I do?' It was so pitiful that both my wife and I could hardly keep back the tears. Then he would remember more sins and bring them out. Finally, he said, 'My heart is open before God: I can remember nothing more to confess: the way is now clear to reach God. Thank God! Thanks be to Jesus for His blood which forgives and saves!' Then he got to his feet and sang, 'I once was a prodigal'. How he leaped, danced, sang, praised, and shook hands all round.

"Teacher Gbadi appeared unmoved when most of his friends got through to blessing. He is a strong man, and would not be easily moved. But one day he went under the power of the Spirit. He rolled on the floor, despite the fact that he had a nice white shirt and shorts. (It is common to see proud teachers dressed immaculately rolling in the dust and mud, quite unconcerned with their appearance.) He agonized for a long time without making a confession. It was during our morning meal that we saw about four or five men carrying him to our veranda. Then he suddenly found the strength to start his confession. First he covered his face with his hands, but he ended up by lying on his back, hands at his sides, confessing his sins with a loud voice and crying to God for mercy. He looked like a man who was absolutely beaten, conquered. Then he jumped to his feet shouting, 'My heart is free! Thank God! Hallelujah!' Gbadi had become a new creature in Christ Jesus; but he was of no use in the schoolroom for a few days. Instead of teaching the children, he would be delving into the New Testament or hymnal, and simply could not bring himself sufficiently down to earth to teach class.

"It is impossible to record everything. We could fill pages with testimonies. The wild dancing and singing is more settled now, but the deep joy remains. Children and adults speak to themselves 'in psalms and hymns and spiritual songs, singing and making melody' in their hearts to the Lord.

"Preaching is such a joy now. The simplest teaching is so new to the folk. They are all the time saying, 'This is new to us. We knew the doctrine before, but now we know the power.' Children and adults are not ashamed to walk the streets with their New Testaments in their hands. This means something in a town like Wamba. Most of the teachers are now changing their fancy names to simple New Testament names. Those teaching the kindergarten used to be reluctant to teach Scripture portions. They did it because it was in the curriculum – that was all. Now they do not need reminding!

"One elder from an out-church came under the power of the Spirit as he was returning to his village. He was actually on his cycle, and was so under conviction that he fell off. He got through to wonderful liberty. He has been much used since, and testifies to at least one case of healing. But we have had to warn him against excesses. He seems to have been elated with that case of healing, and has tried his hand at prophecy. There have been a few cases of excess, or perhaps fanaticism would be a better word. Some have had visions and trances which were evidently not of God. We made an open challenge of this. Another began to meddle with engaged couples: 'A voice has told me that you are not to marry this person, but so and so.' But here again we have had no cases of obstinacy. We back up our rebukes and exhortations with Scripture, and hitherto our word has been accepted. One woman who had been blessed went about seeking to lay hands on people and saying she was the Holy Ghost. She was evidently deranged. She was at an out-church, and the pastor had forbidden her to enter the place of worship because of her blasphemies. But when we were visiting there, she sat outside the door and became a nuisance. One of the lady missionaries went to her and said strongly to her, 'Follow me.' She followed her to the rest-house. There she spoke straightly to her, telling her this was of the devil and that she should ask God to deliver her. She made her repeat a prayer. After some time of praying together, the woman became absolutely normal and rejoiced that the Lord had delivered her. We have heard several times since that she is quite all right.

"There have been a few cases of people who have been quite ill to all appearances. But their illnesses have been nothing other than deep conviction of sin. One man was ill and did not eat for three and a half days. The relatives sent to the compound, asking for him to be taken to the hospital. Next day he became suddenly normal and confessed to being under conviction of sin.

"What most of our compound people have received during the revival is their first born-again experience. In the cases of Christians who have been living near to the Lord, they have received a new baptism of the Holy Ghost. Some of those have been almost overcome with joy; others have received a deep burden for prayer for the state of the church or for the lost. One woman, for instance, had been in the girls' school for many years, and later became the head teacher. We all found her reliable, and the girls liked and respected her. She married one of the workmen, and together they were given the charge of a small local church. But she went under 'the whip' of the Holy Spirit. She went away into the church garden by herself, and there she received a wonderful baptism. She returned with a new look on her face. What an instantaneous change takes place in the faces of those who give in to the Spirit! She simply ran upon my wife and threw her arms around her neck and hugged her, which is not usual among the Mabudu people. She said, 'Madame, I have found salvation today; I was never really saved before. Today I have received the Lord Jesus.' 'Where were you saved?' my wife asked her. 'In the church garden.' She had quite a surprising confession to make of evil thoughts, jealousies, wrong attitudes, hypocrisy, debts. What a different woman she is today.

"Several have testified to seeing a great white light. One man called his wife into the bedroom and said, 'Look at that bright light. The room is all lit up. I feel the presence of God here.' She could see nothing and told him so, but he became more and more emphatic. Some have tried to describe the whiteness of the light, but they can't find words to do it. They say the whitest cloth would look dirty by the side of it, and even cotton glistening in the sun would look unclean.

"About a month later three of us went 100 miles to a conference of the Babari tribe. The Lord had already begun to work here. The pastor and his wife had both received a mighty baptism. Neither of them had any 'great' sins to confess, but their joy and power was beyond doubt. It was a conference of church leaders. On Sunday morning the pastor's wife gave an excellent message on Acts 7:49, saying how God had been wandering about for years looking for houses in which to dwell and that now the Holy Spirit had come and was finding lots of places of rest for God. She gave her own testimony of how she had always felt she belonged to God, but there was a distance between them. She loved the Lord Jesus, but found it hard to speak to Him. Now He had come to dwell in her. She spoke with great power and liberty and joy. She appealed to the people to allow the Spirit to break their hearts, to cleanse them and to prepare a place of rest for God. At the close she struck up a chorus with great joy. The singing was good, but lacked enthusiasm. She burst into tears and said, 'You have no real joy: you are bound. You are hiding unconfessed sin. The Lord has a wonderful life of fullness for you, if only you will bend and allow Him to break your hearts.' After the close quite a few went under conviction. We could hear them from our rest-house. One evangelist waited around until he could get me alone. He was called a few times to eat food, but had no desire for it. After a big struggle (with no shakings, for many do not shake, but with plenty of perspiration) he unburdened his heart. He said when he saw us arriving in the car, it seemed as if our faces shone and he feared to come near us. He had seen the same thing on the pastor and his wife. He felt there was a great distance between us, which he could not bridge. He knew what it was: it was his unconfessed sin of lust. Poor Mandei! I can see him now, utterly broken, crying to God for forgiveness and cleansing. Then he broke through to liberty and was soon full of great joy. At the next meeting he gave his testimony. Men and women went under the power at once. Several were so noisy that they had to be carried out. We cannot but praise God for this wonderful visitation.

"A week later we had a week-end conference of out-church workers back at Wamba. From the beginning the Spirit worked mightily. Lots of the compound people were present, and being in a state of blessing, brought a tremendous spirit of conviction upon the meetings. One testimony came from a young man who had been a schoolboy here. He was clever and had gained special teaching certificates, and returned here 'knowing everything'. None of us were really happy about him, but we could not put our fingers on any concrete cause. He told the various ways by which intense conviction came on him. He knew his own sins all right, but could not open his mouth. He fought it for a long time, then under his breath quoted a line of a hymn which says, 'Thy will be done'. Immediately his heart was broken and he opened his mouth. He says he saw his hypocrisy in a new light. He was like a bush native, dressing himself in houseboy's clothes to make people think he was a houseboy! But now he was found out. He was a hypocrite. Three times over he had made professions of repentance, but had received no power. Now he had received power. He had planned on leaving the mission, marrying extra wives, and so on. He had even said, 'The Gospel works all right for white people, but is no good for black.' But no one knew of these things until he had confessed them.

"Another was a young man who had had his ups and downs, but had kept on following the Lord as well as he could. He came forward saying he had fire in his heart and could not rest until he had told his story. He spoke with great vehemence, striking the reading-desk. He said he had gone straight since leaving school, and was now getting experience at an out-church with a view of going to Bible School. He brought out a lot of what we might call lesser sins. And then he began to beat his chest with a violence which made me fear he might hurt himself. It reminded me of the publican and the Gospel. He was trying to say something and could not get it out. I knew his story, as he had spoken to me before the meeting. I stepped behind him and whispered, 'The word you cannot get out is lust; now speak out.' He yelled out the word 'Lust'. Only he knows what it cost him to confess that. The chest beating immediately ceased, but he kept thumping the desk as he talked. He said, 'Evil desires were killing me. I have tried and tried to overcome, but failed. I have never committed adultery, but now I see what Jesus meant when he said desires and works are the same thing. I am under the condemnation of an adulterer, even though I have never actually committed the act.' Then he burst into wonderful praise, saying he knew he was forgiven. He thumped that poor desk until I thought he would surely smash it. (But it has stood many a thump since then.) He then went round various folks asking their pardon. He came to me and said, 'Bwana, you may not remember I owe you some money for palm oil; it is a very old debt. I will run off at once to the village and get the money.' 'Wait until after the meeting,' I told him. But no, he must pay it at once.

"The story of restitutions would make a

volume in itself. The head woman confessed
to pilfering rice from church supplies, not
deliberate stealing, but taking small amounts
over the years with the covering thought, 'I am
the head woman, and as such should have
certain privileges.' How subtle is human
nature. She could not rest until she had
collected a large basketful of rice and returned
it to the church supplies. The wife of one of
our houseboys confessed to taking eggs from
our fowls and presenting them to us as her gift
to our wee son. 'It is not enough to confess
this,' she said; 'I will give an egg for each one
I stole.' Some of the schoolteachers had been
taking small handfuls of ground nuts at planting
time. They had no peace until they had restored
the equivalent. A Christian native had sent us
a gift of a basket of European potatoes. We
were absent when it arrived. The wife of a
houseboy saw the basket and said, 'Give me a
few of those potatoes; they have cost the
missionary nothing, and he would not know
we have taken any.' When she went under the
power of the Spirit, she bought some potatoes
to restore them to us. One man came with a
few francs, saying he had bought a New
Testament nearly twenty years ago. He had not
sufficient money then, but had promised to pay
later. He had gone away saying to himself,

'These white people have plenty of money. Why should they trouble about a few francs?' But now he saw this was a great sin and hastened to pay his debt.

"At one time we had a large selection of restored goods on a table: rice, peanuts, eggs, potatoes, money, plates, dishes, bits of soap, and so on. Although most of the restored things are of no great value, we nevertheless encouraged the folk to make restoration.

"One thing happened at this conference which brought many under the power of conviction. The head teacher over the schoolboys had been through all these weeks of revival. He had brought out a few surface things and had got right with lots of folks on small differences. He is a quiet, unmoved sort of man. While others sing joyfully and wave their arms, or show joy in other ways, he just stands and sings without any sign of emotion. I was watching him in the meeting, and just wondered why he was so stiff. Quite suddenly he threw himself right across the aisle. It was just as if he had been hurled out of a cannon. Covering his face with his hands, he cried and shouted. Finally, we had to carry him to the vestibule. There he brought out a bad story of deceit and hypocrisy and secret dancing. Who would have believed it of Sabu? Again and again we have had proof of those searching words, 'The heart is deceitful above all things, and desperately wicked; who can know it?' It took him a long time to get it all off his chest. Then we brought him back into the church. He immediately stood to testify, and then the place went 'mad with joy'. The meeting went on until a late hour.

"A new experience in praying came to us during this conference. When it was announced that we should have a time of prayer, everybody started praying at the same time. Most of our prayer sessions are like that now. There is amazing power in such meetings. Such praying and such taking hold of God's promises! We have always had good prayer meetings here at Wamba, but this is quite different. There is no confusion. It begins just like the sound of a rising wind, and continues in a low roar until the prayers begin to die away, and it gradually descends to a stillness. Some stand, others sit, others kneel to pray. Sometimes ones or twos would go under conviction and be carried out or dealt with on the spot. The pleading for lost relatives and outside pagans is very touching. A few may allow themselves to get over-excited, but a kind word sets them right.

"During one of the long meetings I came out for a drink of milk. A few followed me out, among them one of our older evangelists. When the others had finished their affairs, he came near. We were alone on the veranda. He began to speak, telling me how God had shown him his heart, and how he had undergone terrible conviction in the meetings. He began to confess hardness, lack of power in witnessing and wrong attitudes. Actually he has been much used in the past to the conversion of many, and has started many a cause for God. Then he began to weep and strike his hands with terrible vigour. How my heart went out to him! He is a very public man, strong in body and mind; I knew by the way he wept he had a bad confession to make. I could not but weep with him. His tears were falling rapidly on the floor. Then he burst out with all his strength, 'I have done it, Bwana. I have done it! You did not know, but I have done it!' He could not bring it out. But at last he said, 'I have committed adultery on three occasions.' I saw afresh the truth of what the natives were now saying; the Holy Spirit is making people confess things which they never would have confessed under flogging or torture. When he had emptied his heart and really taken hold of forgiveness and cleansing, I took him by the hand and walked him back to the church. He went right on to the platform and gave his story.

It cost him a lot. Amid tears and shouting he got it all out. His remorse was terrible, but he eventually got through to joy and praise. I am sure there was joy in heaven at that moment. The singing almost lifted the roof.

"The business meetings of the conference were bathed in oil. There was a wonderful smoothness and oneness of mind. Another fruit of the revival is keenness to witness. Every Sunday we send out teams of four or six to the local churches to tell what God has done for them. Later on we hope really to tackle the pagans. I wish I had a record of short phrases which show the wonderful change so clearly. Here are a few: 'I used to pray like a parrot; now I pray with the understanding.' 'We used to read the Word without knowing what we were reading; now it is as honey because we have received understanding.' 'Our relationship with wife and children is now as different as light from darkness.'

"Maria, the woman I mentioned before who became mad, was very difficult and had to be handled strongly. The case has been a great blessing to us all. We took up the challenge in prayer. The morning meetings were given over to prayer for her deliverance, and became very powerful. We searched the Word for suitable promises, and then claimed them in prayer.

After some days we changed from praying to receiving and praising. The joy after prayer was tremendous. One morning Maria had been very difficult. We had to have people sleeping in her house because she was so uncontrollable. She was sitting on our veranda and closed her eyes. After a moment she said to my wife, 'I have been asleep; now I am healed.' She was perfectly normal in a moment. But later in the day she said, 'I have been mad for three months. The reason is I have loved an unsaved man who has a wife and children. I still love him and will never give him up.' All persuasion could not move her. That same night she became as mad as before. We looked upon this as an assault from the enemy of souls, and we went back to God. Our faith rose quickly, and we maintained our praise. Some days later one of the lady missionaries felt she had a word from the Lord for Maria, and so it proved. It was, 'Forgetting those things which are behind, and reaching forth unto those things which are before.' Maria was asked to repeat the words, and then to ask the Lord to help her to do as the Word said. This she did and changed from that moment, yielding up that awful sin which had kept her bound. It was a wonderful experience for many of our folk who had never before known a real prayer battle."

The senior lady missionary at Wamba summed it all up by saying: "General signs of the blessing received are: (1) a teachable spirit; (2) a really thankful spirit, which is such a change; (3) such wonderful singing, where before they would hardly open their mouths; (4) eagerness to intercede for others. What wonderful days we are living in. We are full of praise to our God for allowing us a share in the revival. We ourselves have been blessed and revived with greater love for souls, greater burden of prayer, new treasures from the Word, and a greater carefulness in our attitude to each other that we may have that love for one another which is the unity of the Spirit."

5

LIKE THE DAY OF PENTECOST

IBAMBI, the headquarter station of the mission, was first opened by C. T. Studd in 1921 among the populous Mabudu tribe, the same tribe as that at the Wamba station, but forty miles to the north. Here is the Central Bible School, the printing press, and a medical centre is now being started for the training of African nurses. It has always been the home of the field leader. In the gardens at the back Mr. Studd's body was laid to rest to await the resurrection morning, and beside it, Mr. Jack Harrison's, who followed him as field leader, and others who have laid down their lives for the Gospel's sake. There are boys' and girls' schools, and in the surrounding area a number of out-churches, several of which have large attendances. In one of these, Imbais, the only revival previously experienced on our field took place some twenty years ago, the story of which has been told in the book by Eva Stuart Watt, *Floods on Dry Ground*.

The mighty working of the Spirit began in Ibambi about the same time as at Wamba, and by the same means as at both Opienge and Wamba, the visit of an evangelist and his wife from Lubutu, where the Spirit had first broken forth among the people.

One of the young missionaries recently out from the homeland wrote on July 15 1953: "We wanted a move of the Spirit here at Ibambi. We wanted to see houseboys get right with God, schoolboys and girls come to the Lord, and workmen doing their work as unto the Lord. We had watched the roof of the new print-shop slowly going on and wondered when it would really be finished. How we longed to see these men doing their work with zeal and joy. So we were glad to welcome into our midst a couple straight from Lubutu – an evangelist and his wife who had been blessed down there. Last Sunday morning we went as usual to the 7.00 prayer meeting. The evangelist's wife was filled with the Holy Spirit, shaking and praising the Lord. It was a shock to us all. We had sat so quiet and proper week by week. One of the schoolgirls confessed afterwards that she thought, 'Why have these people come from Lubutu to spoil our meeting?' Praise the Lord, they did spoil our meeting. In the afternoon the evangelist took it, speaking in the power of the Holy Spirit and with the quiet confidence of those who are led by Him. After he had spoken, he asked us to pray silently. Suddenly at the back we heard a woman's voice crying louder and louder, 'Jesus'. She went on for several minutes. Then another woman fell to the ground under the power of the Spirit. It was awe-inspiring. These were Christian women, and they had seen the Lord. No wonder they cried out and fell to the ground. The Lord filled them to overflowing with joy and the Holy Ghost. There was a quietness about the people as they came out of the meeting. Even the schoolgirls were subdued, and men who had resisted the Lord for years went away in silence. That evening saw the beginning of a work among our people. Schoolgirls went to the lady missionary to confess sins which are almost unbelievable to us, and workmen began to confess to stealing and laziness. This spirit of conviction prevailed throughout the next day. Houseboys began to confess to stealing, and workmen continued to get right with God. The Holy Spirit was brooding over the station. On Monday several said they had been unable to eat or sleep till they got right with God. Some had felt the power of the Spirit in them as though their hearts were burning, and some had shaken under His power. You should see the roof of the printing-shop today. It is nearly finished!"

The field leader and his wife, who were away, returned a fortnight later to rejoice in what God had begun to do. Up till then, the Spirit had been working quietly over the whole compound, and largely outside of meetings, but that night at the meeting, after he had told them a little of what he saw on his visit to Opienge, "the Holy Ghost came down in mighty power", he wrote. "We have never seen anything like it before. Words fail to describe it, but we know something now of what it must have been like on the day of Pentecost. As one prayed, another began to pray, and another, and then the whole congregation together. Such a noise as they poured out their souls in prayer and praise to God. Men, women, boys and girls just drunk with the Spirit, many shaking beyond their control, others throwing themselves on the floor, some leaning, some standing. One man danced about exhorting them to fear God and not hide sin, but his voice was soon drowned in the hubbub. We just stood there amazed, but were not afraid, as we knew the Spirit was working. We just walked about among them, seeking to help where we could, though it was impossible to make oneself heard. If this had not been of God, it would have been terrible, as they were beyond all human control. Although many threw themselves about, or rather were thrown down, yet none was hurt. All this went on for about an hour, and then as it quietened a bit, a hymn was sung and the people dispersed. We got to bed late, but it was not to sleep much, as our hearts were so full of praise."

As the blessing continued through successive days, he wrote again, "Praise His blessed name for all the wonderful things He is doing in our midst these days. As we have been trusting the Lord for years to pour out His Spirit upon us in revival, now we rejoice in the answer. We do not need to be afraid of any manifestations which are strange to us. Strange things have accompanied every true revival, but when the Spirit is allowed full sway He is able to take care of His own work. We need to be continually ready for any revelation He gives. As the enemy seeks to get in, we shall have discernment and be able to recognize his devices. We have certainly seen manifestations we never saw before, but we know the work is of the Spirit because of the outworking of it in a practical way in so many lives. Throughout it all we are seeking to get the teaching home, so that they will really seek Jesus and not just a blessing. We praise God that the teaching we have had on the Word for years is bringing forth fruit. They know what to do, and the Scriptures are being brought to their remembrance by the Spirit. There is no need to say, 'Those who want to be saved stay behind, or stand up.' The Holy Spirit does the work. We do not take charge. The Holy Spirit leads the meeting, and we don't know what is going to happen next. We are so full of joy that God has visited us at last. He has no set way of working, and it seems to come differently in each place. There is continual praise to Jesus and for His precious blood. This makes us sure that it is a work of the Holy Spirit we are seeing. I tremble to think what might have happened if we missionaries had been out of the Spirit and not able to recognize His working. We should have been horrified and sought to put a stop to it at once. One thing in which we rejoice is that in all this movement our African brothers and sisters are coming to the fore. God is using some of them in a wonderful way. We missionaries are only in the background, and yet we are with them in all that God is doing."

In Ibambi the blessing came in three distinct waves. First, as already related, was upon the station people and schools. The second, a few weeks later, came upon the Bible School. "The students were out on trek when the fire fell at Ibambi," wrote the field leader. "News travels quickly in Congo; and they heard about it as they were on their way back. The minds of some were made up before they arrived. 'I have no sin to confess', one had said, and another, 'Aren't I a Bible School student? There is nothing wrong with me.' But others arrived in fear and trembling, for the Holy Spirit had already begun His work of convicting of sin. Can we ever forget that first Fellowship meeting when the Bible School students were intermingled with the crowd, some thinking they wouldn't be noticed? The Holy Ghost singled them out. HE is no respecter of persons. Here was a woman on her knees weeping her heart out; there a man confessing his sins before God. While this was taking place, another woman had a vision; she saw a list of her sins written on paper. She looked down it, and said, 'Yes, Lord, I am ready to forsake this and this' – then she came to the last: the lust of the flesh. There was a battle raging inside. 'I can't let that go,' she said. She knew the awful confessions she would have to make. What would her husband say? What would the missionaries think? She struggled and fought, but Jesus won, and the list was cleansed away in the precious Blood. Hallelujah! What a victory! What contrition! What tears! What joy! The bells in Heaven must have been ringing out the wonderful news that Ana had 'put off...the old man, which is corrupt according to the deceitful lusts...and put on the new man (Christ Jesus) which after God is created in righteousness and true holiness.' The husband had a new wife; he forgave all, and his own heart leaped for joy.

"During the next few days, God dealt with each student in turn. One woman had hatred in her heart towards others. As she confessed this, the Holy Ghost threw her down. She went flat out on the cement floor. As she rose to her feet, joy flooded her soul; she walked up and down praising the Lord and thanking Him for the work He had done in her heart. The next day she had no recollection that she had fallen. One could multiply stories of restitutions which had to be made, incompatibility between husbands and wives, neglect of Quiet Times, etc. When all were through, we had a real baptism of joy; the whole station heard, and many came around to see what was happening. It was joy unspeakable and full of glory. We had a new Bible School; head knowledge was now becoming heart experience; songs of praise arose to the Throne day and night. We seemed to be wrapped around with the very Presence of the Lord. It seemed but a step to reach the Glory. Prayer sessions were now alive with power, concern for loved ones, backsliders, pagans. What a volume of prayer ascended, mingled with tears, as they poured out their hearts to the Lord, some on their knees, others prostrate. Another was in such agony of soul (because he is the only one out of nineteen relations who is saved) that it took two strong men to hold him down; the power of the Holy Ghost was so strong upon him, the form just shook under him. We have never been in such prayer meetings before; praying together seems to release power. As the Holy Ghost lays the burden of intercession upon them, so He prays through them."

The third wave of blessing came when the local evangelists and out-church leaders were in for a conference, which was extended several days.

"Our meetings have been long," the field leader wrote.

"We have not had much time for meals, and miss several hours of sleep every night, yet we are not extra tired, but are almost more full of joy than we can contain. On Sunday our early morning prayer meeting lasted over two hours. We did not come out of the mid-morning meeting until 4.00 p.m., and then the last one went on till 11.00 p.m. The other days were similar."

One who was visiting the field from the home-end wrote: "I cannot describe the singing, the joy, the music that came forth from all sections of the station. Some nights we were up until after 2.00 a.m., and awake shortly after 4.00 a.m.; we wondered if the people sang all night through. Some nights they didn't sleep, for there was a spirit of prayer for those of the out-church leaders and wives who were not through. This continued on for five days, wave upon wave of joy, then the burden of prayer, until there were only two who had not yielded. It was a terrible day, after days and nights of prayer, when these two again refused the light. I had not witnessed weeping and heartbrokenness of men, big men, before. They lay face down on the floor and wept; they stood with their arms about one another, the tears streaming unheeded down on to the floor. The burden tore at you, until you were sore and weary. I know now what real intercession is, and the vast difference between prayer and intercession. You feel you could die unless the Lord answers. This continued on all day, we didn't eat, we didn't leave the church. Finally, the evangelist Danga stood and spoke with tears still flowing, saying that all had been done that could be done for these two; the Lord showed him that our joy should not be hindered, but to leave the two with Him. As he spoke those words, we all felt a release. Then followed days that cannot be described. The joy was so intense, people hardly knew what to do with themselves. Their outlet was singing."

The climax of the conference was a wonderful communion service, led by the African pastors.

"There were bursts of praise and song such as you never heard", wrote the field leader.

"Each tribe sang in their own language in turn, dancing and flinging up their arms in ecstasy and praise. Anyone coming in from outside would have said we had gone quite mad! I can just imagine how dear old Bwana (C. T. Studd) would rejoice to see this, and know he will be rejoicing in glory over it. We went on singing and praising for a long time. At the end of one meeting a wonderful thing happened, yet I suppose we should not say that, because it is only what happened at Pentecost, and this is our Pentecost. I made a few announcements about the next meeting, but one of our two visitors from the home-end who did not know the African languages, heard all I said in English, yet I had spoken in Swahili. When I told them of this at the next meeting, a Spirit-filled African woman got up and said that twice, when she had been praying with us in our house before some of the meetings, she had understood all that we prayed, even though we had prayed in English, a language of which she did not know a word."

One missionary describes what God was doing those days as first prostration with the awful conviction of sin; then praising God for the blood of Jesus; then praying, agonizing for souls; then preaching, getting out to witness and lead others to a saving knowledge of Jesus; and finally, purging, as one or another rises up and points out folk whom he knows by the Spirit are not right with God, and pleads with them to get right before it is too late.

6

THE HOLINESS OF GOD

ONE of the missionaries at Ibambi, who has been over twenty-five years on the field, gives us a glimpse of what lay behind this revival.

"To think that we've ever been privileged to live through these days of revival blessing," she writes.

"It is beyond anything we had imagined. We have longed, prayed, cried, agonized for revival, and God has done the 'exceeding abundantly'. We are only in its beginnings, for judgement begins where God says it does – at the house of God. He has been setting His house in order, purifying, cleansing, empowering by the blood and Spirit, now He will turn to the heathen, and who shall abide the day of His coming? Our people have had a revelation of the sinfulness of sin and the holiness of God, and they know now, not in their heads but in their hearts, that 'without holiness no man shall see the Lord'. Before it was, as it were, the missionaries' interpretation of the Word, now it is the Holy Ghost convincing them of the truth. Scores and scores have been absolutely broken before the cross. The Holy Ghost has dug deep and brought to light the filth which had been buried away for years. There was no escaping, they had to call a spade a spade, big and so-called little sins had to be classified together. In the light of the cross and a holy God everything looked vile – bad thoughts, criticisms against one's neighbour, pride in every form, lust in the thought life, worldliness in dress, etc. But as the testimonies have been given, what joy, what peace, what radiance, what ecstasy, as the Holy Ghost came in and took possession. As testimony after testimony poured forth, so there was a releasing more and more of the power of the Holy Ghost until we were wild with joy. I fully understand now why David danced before the ark! I for one have been caught right up into the glory of the whole thing and thought I would burst with sheer joy. Away back in 1935 God gave me Isaiah 60 as a promise of revival. I have the date written at the side of this chapter. Others have probably got their promises too, for many have been pouring out their hearts to God for revival. We were getting desperate. Since I returned from furlough the pressure from the enemy has been terrific, we have never known anything like it. In January, during a quiet week-end in preparation for a coming ministry, my husband and I took the book *Rees Howells, Intercessor* with us. I finished the last few chapters when sitting in a small mud house where it was quiet. My spirit was overwhelmed within me. As I thought of all that wonderful life had accomplished, it just created a great longing to know for myself something more of this life of intercession. I went to my husband, and we talked together again of the need of revival, and then we got to prayer. The burden was terrific. We told God we didn't mind where revival began, or through whom, but revival we must have, we were desperate. Others we knew were desperate also. When news came from Lubutu that revival had started, we found it began that very weekend. No wonder we had felt the urgency of prayer.

"Now we have just had the third wave of revival in Ibambi, and it has nearly overwhelmed us. I have felt the tide of blessing rising up in my own soul. I wondered before the revival came here why God insisted, on two occasions when I was praying alone in my bedroom, that I should get flat on the floor before Him. I told Him that it would dirty my dress, for you know what our Congo floors are like! He quietly insisted, and won. I didn't know that He was putting me into practice for this last week, but I can see it all now.

"The closer one approaches to God, the deeper the realization of His holiness and His standard. Bwana (C. T. Studd) used to say, 'How much sin can you do and get to heaven?' If no sin can enter into heaven, then it has got to be dealt with beforehand. The One who has made the standard so high surely has made the provision through His beloved Son to reach it. Why should we be afraid to say that Jesus can cleanse from all sin and keep us cleansed? The blood which can cleanse from nine-tenths can surely cleanse the remaining one-tenth. John surely knew what he was writing in 1 John 3:6. It is startling but true, so true that it is time we started to believe it and act upon it. The devil will always bring in arguments to throw dust in our eyes and get home the thing which he knows is going to keep us anaemic and powerless, namely, 'You have a fallen nature, therefore as long as you are in the body, you will sin.' The devil always was a liar, and always will belittle what Jesus did for us on the cross. I see in my beloved Saviour One who died to make me like Himself. He was without sin, therefore if I will really let Him do the work He wants to do in my heart and life, then He can make and keep me free from the cursed thing which nailed Him to the cross. I can't lower the standard just because I haven't reached it, neither can I ever disbelieve that which is written so clearly in God's Word. If by faith we let Him live His life through us, He the sinless One, then He will produce the holiness we read of in God's Word. This revival has taught me that we can assent to an awful lot with our minds, and have reservations in our hearts. God is far more interested in the latter. We get no more and climb no higher than our desires. Who am I to be writing about holiness? I need to get there myself. I am such a long way from being what I ought to be. However, like Paul, I press on toward the goal.

"After writing the first pages of this letter, I went over to the usual Wednesday prayer meeting with the Bible School women, and lo and behold, one of the students spoke on the text, 'Be ye holy, for I am holy', together with Hebrews 12: 14. She said, 'God can make you holy because He says so, and it is up to you to keep holy by watching to see that nothing comes into the life to make it unholy.' She used an illustration of a basket of peanuts which is kept in reserve for planting. She said, 'If you are not watchful, the rats will get at it and make havoc, then it is wasted. The rats are like sin, keep them out, be watchful.' I am sure thousands will be swept into the kingdom. Daily we hear of souls being saved, many are under conviction of sin, many fear. It will spread – even the natives have got that assurance – through Africa to the uttermost parts."

7

THE SPIRIT FALLS
ON THE LEPERS

OTHER mission centres experienced the same mighty movings of the Spirit. The nearest to Ibambi was the leper and maternity centre at Nebobongo, which was visited by a team of witness.

"Hearts were full of expectancy", wrote one of the missionaries there: "at least the hearts of those who were right with God, whereas others were desperately afraid and went away for the week-end without permission. Some even said they would not bring out their sin, though the Holy Ghost came.

"However, there were the same scenes of terrific breakings, cleansings, and transformations as at Ibambi, and then the joy, joy, intoxicating joy. Numberless souls got right with God and through to the fullness of the Spirit. Lepers and clean folk all got mixed up together; no barriers, falling on the ground and around our necks, witnessing to the great work God had done in their hearts. For a few nights no one went to bed, but were out all night singing and seeking the lost. Ours is a new station, with a new people, who have a new outlook on life."

Two of our home-base workers, husband and wife, who represent the leper work in the homelands, were visiting the field at this time. The wife's vivid account of what they saw, particularly among the lepers and in other places, is worth quoting here at length.

"On the way out from England we heard of revival on our southern-most station of Lubutu, but we were not too much impressed; for in America the word revival has often been used in reference to evangelistic meetings. Upon our arrival in the Congo, we realized the burden upon the hearts of the missionaries, and the African leaders as well, for their people. Many were professing with their mouths to love the Lord, but their lives were not consistent. Many cases of sin were being uncovered. For some time there had been much prayer that God would do a new thing and send revival. So there had been an expectancy in hearts. There were good crowds at meetings, and people seemed to listen well, but there was no conviction of sin, even though they could give all the answers. The burden of prayer upon many hearts was for the cleansing, purifying Spirit to come and work. But now, the prayers of years were being answered by one mighty stroke of God's hand. We heard of wonderful things happening, and we had a desire to go and see.

"In due course we arrived at Lubutu and began to see. Here was joy! Such a contrast from the Christians up country; these people simply vibrated with life. The singing was a revelation, for they seemed to have a new song, and new power to sing it. Then we heard them in prayer, not just one voice at a time, but all at once the entire congregation praying; and as I opened my eyes, I saw even little children closed in with the Lord in prayer. They wept and pleaded with the Lord for souls. I had never witnessed such agonizing before the Lord. Every ear was tuned to the messages. One of the evangelists who exhorted them in their walk broke down and wept as he praised the Lord for the new day for them. As we travelled back towards our main station, we stopped at out-churches along the way; and the people were saying, 'The Spirit of God has come.' Others said, 'We want the same work in our midst.' It was just dusk when we arrived at our Wamba station, but we knew what had happened, for the people came running, and the joy on their faces told the story. Way into the night we listened to the wonderful things the Lord is doing, and all about us we could hear singing and praying. The next morning we went on to Ibambi; all along the way the 'fire' had fallen. And surely it was true, for we walked into our station to find our people as 'them that dream'. The greetings and their singing were beyond words, and we could only stand and weep for joy at the transformed lives before us. We found missionaries and Africans alike, simply bubbling over, and all trying to tell us of God's working in their hearts. Hallelujah! The Spirit of God had come in power to Congo, and we were in the very midst of it.

"The days that followed our return to Nebobongo leper station were wonderful beyond words. For there was hardly a moment when someone was not coming to confess to having taken something, or with some wrong they wanted to make right, or to ask permission to go and make restitution, so that nothing would remain to hinder the Spirit's working in their lives. Night after night we were in meetings where we saw over and over again the same working of the Spirit. As people witnessed, telling how God worked in their hearts, some would go down under conviction and were soon rejoicing in the Lord; others would be saved. The meetings were crowded out, also unbelievers would flock to watch from the outside of the church. Many fell to the ground under conviction who had just come to watch. God was going right to the bottom, leaving nothing unconfessed or hidden. As one confessed, it would uncover sin in another. Their only concern now was to be free from sin.

"Our first Sunday back from the South was spent at one of the big leper camps, taking a number of the station people and lepers with us. These Africans were filled with the Holy Spirit and were on fire. We sang all the way out to the camp, and I couldn't help but notice the looks upon the faces of the folks whom we passed on the road. How we praised Him that we were inside the 'Hallelujah' bus, knowing we were saved and filled with His Spirit, instead of being alongside the road, wondering what it was all about. We arrived just after the services had started; the meeting was immediately turned over to the team we brought with us. One by one, these Africans gave their testimonies amidst bursts of song and praises to Him; and we shall never forget the picture of these lepers sitting with their hands clasped in front of them, their eyes glued on the faces of the revived Africans as they heard how God had worked in these hearts. Then came a time of prayer. As we bowed our heads and closed our eyes, one started to pray, then another, then like the soft rain over the forest trees, others joined in until, like a sudden rush of rain, every voice was lifted in prayer. The praying turned to weeping, then sobbing, and wailing – then it happened!

"I found myself standing wringing my hands and weeping as the sound of cries all about us became greater and greater. A woman on my left slipped off her stool and lay as though dead. I turned to look at the other missionaries, and they, too, had pale faces as we looked upon the scene before us. Then it seemed like bedlam had broken loose, for people all over were falling from their seats and crying out in agony of conviction. The missionaries and African leaders moved about among the people listening, and all were pouring out sin and crying for mercy and forgiveness. The first woman was now crying and confessing sin. God was dealing deep and sure; no one else mattered to these souls now, and many confessions were being heard only by the Lord. We knew the Spirit was in control, for we felt His presence in our midst. Many faces were uplifted and wet with tears. Some were being held by as many as six persons as they writhed about in their agony. The one young lad in whom I was interested sat motionless, looking wide-eyed all about him;

then it seemed that an unseen hand picked him up from his seat and thrust him upon the ground, then began to dig out that which is an abomination to the Lord. He cried with a loud voice as he began to pour out the terrible sin in his heart. One of the men kneeling beside him also went over on the ground in agony of soul. Then, like a drunken man, the lad finally got to his feet and began to praise the Lord with tears still flowing. I watched him as the transformation took place and as the light of heaven came over him; his face was a picture of joy and release, as he praised the Lord over and over again, saying 'Thank you, thank you, Jesus.'

"As we watched, it seemed that every sin must be confessed and brought out into the light, for the searchlight of the Holy Spirit was going deep into every recess of the heart. Only then did release from the agony of conviction come. Then, staggering to their feet, they praised the Lord with loud voices, shouting, 'Hallelujah,' and 'Thank you, Jesus.' A young mother near us quietly went over on the ground, and as she went over, someone reached for her babe. She began to confess in a loud crying before the Lord. Many standing outside had come to watch, some with fear upon their faces, others looking on with open-mouthed amazement, and others even turned and fled. The young lad was still staggering about with his hands in the air, saying 'Asanti, Asanti', and as I watched another change came over him, and down he went, this time on his knees, weeping and praying, not for himself, but for others who had not as yet yielded to the Spirit. He went over and fell on his knees before a woman and pleaded with her to get right with the Lord. Then he moved on to another and another, his tears falling unheeded to the floor.

"We saw this repeated over and over again, and many were now on their faces weeping for others. One woman went over and spoke to a man who had been sitting like stone through all this. Then she came back and sat down, when all at once she went over on her face, giving a death wail for this man. I looked at the man, and all at once he went over and he was in terrible agony as God dealt with him. He was a big man, but he, too, finally began to tell out his sins, and then came free. His rejoicing was great.

"We do not really know how many people yielded to the Spirit that day, but we were there from ten in the morning to four in the afternoon, and the Spirit was working all the time. We were not aware of the passing of time, even forgetting the lunch we brought with us. God was dealing with the Christians, first, a burden of prayer for their own need, then terrifying conviction of sin, then release and praise, and finally a burden of prayer for others. We were actually living in Acts 2:2, from this day and on, hearing the sound from heaven of the mighty rushing wind, as the people began to pray; then the fear and amazement of the unbelieving, and the mocking; then the 13th verse, 'these men are full of new wine', and the glorious truth of verse 17, 'I will pour out of my spirit upon all flesh'. Many times we were shaken as in Acts 4:31. Timid and fearful women were being made bold in the Lord; and stammering men began speaking fluently; and little children began giving forth the Word made alive and real to them.

"In the months that followed we moved about from station to station, seeing the Spirit come in all His power, transforming hundreds of lives. What glorious days! What a wonderful God, who loves us so much that He would come and deal with us so faithfully. We saw a deaf woman's hearing restored as she was filled with the Spirit; a little boy made whole, one whose little body had been hopelessly twisted; sick people raised from their beds; some near death, raised up; and most wonderful of all, those who had been backslidden and away from the Lord for years came back because the Spirit of God drew them. One fact that impressed us very much is that when God put a burden upon the heart for those who had gone astray, these souls returned and came through gloriously. This is real travail for souls.

"At our Ibambi station where our Bible School is located, we saw tremendous things happen. Our field leader returned from one of the stations where the Holy Spirit had come, and told the crowd what he had seen and heard. Later when they went to prayer, bedlam broke loose, although they could not account for how it happened, as the Spirit came down upon the whole congregation. People were stretched out all over the floor screaming out their sins. They just fell, and not one was hurt or bruised. This is an amazing thing, for the head printer seemed to fly through the air over the backs of the people, landing on the floor, where he began crying out his sin. Day and night, God dealt with the 400 people on the station, until all were filled with the Holy Spirit. Some of the building on the station that had been dragging along for months, was completed in three days. The schoolboys came asking for special prayer just before leaving on their month of vacation, saying they knew what temptations they would be facing when they returned to their villages.

The challenge was put to them, that if God has really met them and filled them with His Holy Spirit, they would be able to stand against all temptation. When we said goodbye to these boys we were tempted to wonder if all the 220 would return and still be praising the Lord. The day they were to return was exciting, for by nightfall, not only 220 boys returned still praising the Lord, but thirty new students had also come with them. What rejoicing that night around the fires as they recounted the happenings of the past month. And we knew by the shining faces that all was well, as they told of some of the wonderful ways the Lord had sustained them in times of temptation. The Lord had not only kept them, but hundreds of souls had also come to the Lord through them. This was also true of the girls on the station. When we came to Sunday dinner we heard praying in the little prayer room set aside for the boys. I asked who was there, and the missionary said it was a group of the boys. But when we returned that night for supper, I again heard praying and weeping. I again asked who was in the prayer room, and again the answer, 'The boys are still in there praying.' There was no monitor with them, but they had a burden for the new boys who had come back with them to school. All day they had fasted and prayed that God would work in the hearts of the new students. I thought, when boys in their early teens spend a day fasting and praying for the lost, something is bound to happen. Some were saying, 'Why haven't you taught us these wonderful truths before?' The only answer is that now their eyes and ears are open to see and hear. Others have said, 'We thought that this Christianity was only for the white man, for we could never live up to this standard.' But now, eyes are open to see this wonderful Christianity is for all who hear and believe.

"No more do people straggle into the meetings; they run, they are there before the drums beat, singing and rejoicing. Everyone comes expecting God to work. Newcomers are in almost every meeting. No longer are the meetings only of an hour's duration; sometimes many hours go by, and we are not conscious of time or the need of food. The first meeting is generally at six-thirty in the morning, and many times we have had our first food in the middle of the afternoon or early evening. Singing and praying continues on through the night. The Lord let us experience what these Africans go through day after day as they pray, for we have had to confess that we knew nothing of such travail for souls as we witnessed daily. It seemed that if the Lord didn't answer our prayers we would surely die. Our bodies ached with the burden He put upon us, but we saw the Lord move and work in a way we had all longed to see.

"One of our boys sat at his sewing-machine, working. He had been singing, but now his song had turned to weeping. One must hear that kind of weeping to understand the depths of the burden behind it. One of our missionaries went to him and found the Lord had laid a burden upon his heart for some of the boys who had been at school through the years and had gone astray.

"Early one morning, we were awakened by terrible sobbing as one of the Bible Students came for prayer for deliverance from a temper which had been a detriment in his service to the Lord. He sobbed his way through to glorious victory.

"Another young man went to his day's work from the early morning meeting where the Lord had blessed; and as he was preparing the washing, he looked at the clothes and said, 'My, this is a large washing today.' The next moment he was down on his face under conviction, and soon made his way to the missionary and fell at her feet, sobbing as he told of the awfulness of the realization of coming from the presence of the Lord, to murmuring in his heart over a bit of work.

"Sometimes the cost of obedience is great. One man, a Christian, had a large plantation of wine palms. He had long since ceased drinking himself, but the Lord now convicted him of making wine to sell to others. When he saw it was wrong for him to even sell it, he cut down the whole grove of trees. Each tree is valued at about $4.00.

"There were those who tried to resist, but to no avail. One man was seen to hug his knees with his arms to keep from shaking and falling over. Another ran to the post in the church, wrapping his legs and arms about it, but he also went down. Others declared they would not confess their sins, but when God put His hand on them, out it came. Some do not like the manifestations. Some want revival in an orderly way. Some of us were fearful in the beginning, for we have come from reserved backgrounds and were afraid of anything out of the ordinary. Reports in John Wesley's Journal give a picture of just what we have been witnessing here in the Congo during these last months.

"The African now has a burden for his own people. All who are able, go out over the week-end, preaching and telling what God has done. One Sunday we saw a large group of men

from the station starting out with their Bible
bags thrown over their shoulders, singing as
they went. Next, came a group of men and boys
on bicycles, and finally, a group of women with
babes on their hips, and their Bibles; God's
army was on the march! That evening,
Hallelujahs rang over the compound as these
returned, weary but happy, for souls had come
through and mighty victories had been won that
day."

8

THE HARDEST STATION OF ALL

PERHAPS the greatest miracle of all to those who know the field is that the Spirit should have broken through at the Egbita centre. Although the work is over twenty years old, it has always been a hard and dry district, with little response from the Meje tribe who live in that area, compared with the response in so many neighbouring tribes. It was in the same month of July that the Lord broke through.

"While three separate groups were having evening prayers," wrote the missionary in charge, "the Holy Ghost fell on all meetings simultaneously, and terrific scenes followed. I was glad to have visited Opienge and Lubutu beforehand, so was somewhat prepared, but what we witnessed was frightening at first, as souls were struck down in agony. Folks said they saw all their sin as clearly as if written down before them. The meeting went on till 2.30 a.m., but others who had held out came to the house at 3.00 a.m. crying for help. The following day similar things happened. When prayer was called for, the whole congregation rose to its feet as one man, and broke out in prayer and strong crying with tears before the Lord. Each was concerned with his or her own need. We had never witnessed anything so moving in our lives before. Numbers hung on to us whites and nearly pulled us to the ground, craving to be heard and asking forgiveness for all sorts of grievances. The Spirit has hit hard on the pastors, evangelists, and elders for being below standard with only selfish motives. It is true the dry bones can live, hallelujah! God has done in a few days things we had never seen in twenty years of labour, but one realizes too that nothing has been lost of all the effort of sowing and praying. It is as though the Lord has reaped in a day. We found dry-eyed folk never seemed to get through, but all who literally cried to the Lord with broken hearts soon had assurance and joy. It was the same in a local conference with out-church Christians, many straightening up their lives. Some have cut down their wine palms, an unheard of thing for a Meje to do, but what a testimony to the pagans around! All we four whites are in full unity too in this moving of the Spirit, which has made it so easy for Him to work. New life, new Bible, new souls all praising the Lord!"

An evangelist who is taking the teacher training course at Egbita testified with joy to answered prayer. His child, about two, had never been able to walk properly. A doctor diagnosed it as a dislocated hip at birth, but it would have to wait about five years before there could be an operation. But the evangelist was reminded that God could heal without the doctor's help, so he and his wife began to pray. Some days later they noticed the child running around quite normally. The doctor examined him and found him quite all right. There was great rejoicing at what the Lord had done.

The Spirit fell upon our northernmost station, at Malingwia among the Ababua tribe, through the visit of some missionaries and Africans. Though the newest centre, there had been an unusual touch of God upon the work from its beginnings, with flourishing out-churches, a thriving central station, many saved, and some pillars of the church. But as the news reached them of the visitation of the Spirit, hearts became hungry and "our people were largely prepared for revival", wrote the station leader. "We had absolute unity among all the missionaries, who were also largely prepared by letters.

"At the first meeting," he continued, "all were deeply touched by the words of the missionaries, but still more so by the obvious difference in the lads with them from Ibambi.

In the afternoon service a heavy storm came up. Usually there would have been fidgeting, but today complete stillness. Then the first move came. The whole congregation stood and cried out to God. One young woman (well known for petty thieving, though unacknowledged by herself) fell backwards like a babe in arms, under tremendous conviction of sin. Another crawled up to the front on hands and knees. The next morning, however, there was a deadness in the meeting. One lad tried to urge them on, but we restrained him, as we knew God was working in many hearts in conviction."

"Monday seemed like drought after the Sunday downpour," added the wife of the station leader. "Why? What had happened? We divided into groups, boys, girls, station workmen, etc., to seek the Lord. We felt so helpless, we hardly knew what to do, or how to set about things. But Zecheriah 12: 10: 'I will pour upon them ... the spirit of grace and of supplications, and they shall look upon ME whom they have pierced, and they shall mourn ... and be in heaviness . . .' Tremendous intercession poured forth, yet strangely enough I could get under no burden for the boys – only for the men and women. I told the lads this, of my heart-aching burden for their parents, I pleaded with them to open their hearts, 'Don't be stiff-necked. Break. Break.' I could get no farther; I broke down and wept, and wept. I have never known such tears, such agony of tears, as broke from my burdened heart. The little boys broke down, they were standing, or lying on the ground, weeping, weeping, pouring out their hearts before God. The big lads hardened their hearts, stiff-necked, unmoved, and unmovable (though now they are gloriously through also and deeply blessed with all the rest of us). Then the break came – a great and mighty break among the parents. First amongst the men. They just poured out of the church, an army of praising men, dancing for joy. But – no women. Travail as never before came upon me. I thought my heart would break. I pleaded with the men even in the midst of all their mighty joy: 'Stop singing! Be real. Look at your wives. Go and find your partner. Get in your houses, get right between yourselves.' I could hardly speak to them for the fullness of my own heart and my own choking tears. We wept in Holy Ghost desperation and travail. (You cannot work up such tears and travailing: it simply comes down upon you. It is the Holy Ghost travailing in birth through you.)

"A fortnight later we had our second

women's conference. Last year 100 came, but this year the Lord brought over 200 along. A new house was being built, and was to be roofed and finished during the conference. We asked the women whether we should have the spiritual work first, and afterwards get on with the house; or whether we should get to work first, and afterwards to prayer. They chose the latter, being very keen to get on with the house. But the next day they came and said, 'No, we must have the Spirit's work first!' And when they came, the rain of the Holy Ghost just poured down upon them. It was simply wonderful, beyond description. It was like the reports in the Wesley journals. There were no messages, the women were just smitten down to the ground on all sides, falling, writhing in terrible agony. They seemed to see all their life pass before them like a cinema; they truly saw hell and feared. The majority were born-again souls, but over and over again we heard the testimony in the days that followed: 'If we had died in our sins, we'd have gone to hell!' They knew in experience that a sinning soul is in danger of hell-fire, whether saved before or not. And oh, the power, the mighty cleansing power, of the Blood. Faces glowed and shone, as by a lamp within. Two hundred native women filled with the Holy Spirit! The work went ahead afterwards like a whirlwind, and the witness to the mighty power of Calvary, and the indwelling radiating power of the Holy Spirit has gone forth into the whole district."

To this one of the younger women missionaries adds: "How God spoke to the women in the church about jewellery, earrings, etc. A young woman, wife to one of the houseboys, had gone to a nearby field to seek the Lord. It was one week after the Holy Spirit had 'suddenly come to His temple', and people were seeking the Lord at all times and in many places. Almost immediately this young woman, wearing jewellery, went into a trance or had a vision. Her ears and ear-rings grew so big and became so heavy that she was absolutely imprisoned by them, not able to turn around or move forward. At the same time her two hands and wrists were fixed together in front of her, burning away as in a fire. Just at that moment Someone stood by her side, clothed in white apparel, and told her to open the Bible at 1 Timothy 2:9-15 and at 2 Peter 1:12-13. Just then her husband arrived on the scene, and recognizing that his wife was oblivious to anything around and at the same time needing help, began to ask her what had come to her. She asked him to open these passages of Scripture and read them to her, for she herself could not yet read. When later over two hundred women gathered on the station for their annual conference, God mightily dealt with all through this vision. One by one, they took off their ear-rings and beads and bangles and jewellery of every kind or sort, and one by one brought them out to the front and put them into a hat, which soon was filled with 'costly array' – only to be thrown afterwards into a deep pit."

There had been a special burden on the missionaries that husbands and wives should get through together, because the average African couple has little of love and home-life as we know it. The fruits of that were seen on Thursday, which was "the glory day" in the meetings. Wives and husbands stood on the platform weeping together with arms around each other. Others were testifying together to the great joy and love God had given, as they had broken unitedly before Him. One woman stood with her husband saying, "Now I love my husband like a child," for love of children is great, but love for husbands much less common. And at the end of the week one wrote, "As we looked out on the sea of shining faces and spotted various ones we had almost despaired of and feared would never be saved, we thrilled to see them 'lifting up holy hands in prayer', as they instinctively do when praying and praising." As the evangelists and out-church leaders were about to return home, they gathered for a final early morning meeting. "However, the heavens opened and glory streamed down upon us, and the meeting lasted from six-thirty to ten-thirty. Station couples, husbands and wives, filled the front of the church, testifying to the definite call of God to this dark area or that needy place. Then young couples, who are mostly former schoolchildren now married with the beginnings of families, came out, saying God had called them to Bible School."

9

SOME FINAL CONCLUSIONS

THE object of this narrative has not only been to relate the facts to the glory of God, but also to learn valuable lessons from those who have had the responsibility of being under-shepherds of God's flock at a time when heaven has drawn near and the veil been rent in twain. A few final comments may also be of value.

The first is this. The floods have been poured upon prepared ground. From the days when C. T. Studd and his co-workers first found themselves among a people who made easy outward response to the Gospel, it burned like a fire in his bones that only holiness becomes God's house, and without holiness no man shall see the Lord. As a result, the people have had it driven home to them with all the authority of Scripture that repentance towards God, in the completest sense of renunciation of all sin, must precede a living faith toward our Lord Jesus Christ; and that cleansing in the blood and regeneration by the Spirit is demonstrated to be genuine only when they produce continued holiness of life, a love of righteousness, and a hatred of iniquity. Through these thirty-five years that standard has never been lowered, thousands have the Scriptures in their hands, and among them have arisen holy African men and women of God whose sanctified lives have adorned their teaching. Therefore the Holy Ghost has come to a people who can recognize sin as sin, and who at once know the blessed remedy in the blood of Christ and the sanctifying power of the Spirit. They were a prepared people.

Then again there was a prepared missionary body. "Thy people shall be willing in the day of Thy power", wrote the Psalmist. But should we be? For when He does come in power, He does His "strange work", as the prophet said. Unless He first had His missionary servants walking so closely to Him themselves, holy men and women, how could they have stood the sight of these consuming fires, these "everlasting burnings" which they have been witnessing? There have been confessions and breakings, meltings and revival among the missionaries too; but in the main, praise God, those burning fires of conviction, repentance, and cleansing had been at work through the years in their lives, causing them to keep short accounts with God, walking in the light as He is in the light. Because of this, when these terrible convictions have come like a tornado on the churches, the missionaries have been able to recognize them as the holy fire of God which had been constantly burning in themselves, and have welcomed them and co-operated with the Holy Ghost. They and some of the African brethren have been, thank God, vessels already sanctified and meet for the Master's use, when the day of His power came like their tropical rainstorms.

It has required discernment and steadiness. None but the pure in heart who see God, poised in the Spirit, walking as He walked, with their senses exercised by reason of use to discern both good and evil, could have welcomed the reality of such emotional upheavals, and seen calmly and clearly through the contortions and cryings, the fallings, jumpings, and dancings, and sometimes the extravagances, to the pure stream of the Spirit flowing beneath. Maybe the very reading of these experiences will exercise some of us readers; but they judge us, not we them. Those who love the Saviour and the washing of regeneration and renewings of the Holy Ghost will rejoice with a full heart, and covet earnestly the same in their own spheres, in whatever form He comes. It may be easy for others of us, who maybe are not so prepared to face the white light of God's perfection, and the condemnation of everything short of that standard in our lives, to fail to recognize the impact that the horror of sin and the wonder of the shed blood of Christ ought to have even on our emotional life; and it may be easy to resent and shrink from such scenes as are here described, and to find reason for rejecting the inner reality by objecting to its outward form. But it has been refreshing and illuminating to watch the grace, tenderness, and wisdom given our co-workers on the field in uplifting the fallen as those uplifted themselves by grace, in discerning and challenging a false spirit, in the firm though loving check on extravagances, in keeping the flock in Bible pastures, and on the other hand, to see the humble willingness of the newly-born or revived to accept the word of exhortation.

A few more points are worth noting. We have to face the fact that many in our congregations have only a conversion, but not a regeneration. They repent, but don't experience the power of salvation, and are soon back again in their old sinful habits. How many in these Congo revivals confessed to that. Repent, confess, but not born-again. Are we under-shepherds of flocks often deceiving ourselves? We hope that our members are saved, but we have no inner witness, and we cannot genuinely say that they live as those who are dead to sin and the world, and alive unto God. Are not our congregations choked with dead wood of this kind? And will not God hold us responsible, if through not paying the full price of faithfulness and taking up our cross of possible opposition, we leave them as lost souls in that condition? Shall we not raise up again the standard that a Holy Ghost born person is therefore of necessity holy? Do we not need the same divine dissatisfaction which, as we read here, made some of the missionaries desperate for the unmistakable work of the Spirit?

Then it is noticeable in nearly every case that revival spread through the revived. Life transmits life. That challenges us. It is not sermons on revival from pulpit or platform, but personal revival in the speaker, expounded from the Scripture but illustrated in life and testimony, that transmits revival. If we haven't revived congregations, is it not that we ourselves are not revived? We transmit what we are, not what we say; and we can always share what we have, not what we have not. That is the law of life. It looks from the accounts of these revivals that actually revival is always at the door, always just beneath the surface, for the Reviver has been on earth since Pentecost, only He must be transmitted through one who has Him.

One last question. Does it last and will it last? The best answer comes from the field leader, written twelve months later: "As we look back over the last twelve months, we are full of praise to God for all He has done in hearts. Some failures there have been, but these are few in comparison to the many who have proved the reality of a deep work of the Spirit in their hearts. Disappointments have been mostly among young people, the older ones give much cause for praise and thanksgiving to God. It was certainly Revival we saw last year when the Spirit of God came upon us in such mighty power. The manifestations were of the Spirit and not of the flesh. At Pentecost, as recorded in Acts 2, the fire was seen coming upon the disciples; here it was felt; many testified to a feeling of burning in their hearts. Do we judge the depth and reality of revival by the unusual manifestations we have seen? No, decidedly no. 'By their fruits ye shall know them.' Our people continue to have visions, which are an inspiration to us all, but transformed lives are the greatest recommendation. Hands are doing an honest day's work, which once were limp and unwilling to do anything for Jesus. Yes, our workmen are on the job, singing as they work. There is now no idling, standing about, and wasting time as there was before the Revival. Lips are now ready to give a word of testimony, pass on a short message from God's Word, or sing His praises. Women and girls, who were once shy and reticent, now come boldly forward and make a valuable contribution to our meetings; the air rings again with their Hallelujahs! Our Fellowship meetings are alive; there are always more ready to speak than time allows, even though the usual length of the meeting is from two and a half to three hours. There is always abundance of joy, praise, and prayer, though sometimes the prayer burden is greater than at others.

"If this revival had not been real, it would have fallen to pieces before this, for the enemy of souls has thrown his full weight against it. Never have we had so many onslaughts, never have we had to go through such fiery trials, but our Beloved Lord has been with us through it all.

"Are we satisfied? No, for as yet we have seen no great awakening among the pagans. Some have been saved; every week sinners are coming to the Saviour, including pigmies, but we long for more. God continues to purify and cleanse His Church, then 'the heathen shall know that I am the Lord, saith the Lord God, when I shall be sanctified in you before their eyes.' One of our missionaries had a vision of two fruit trees full of blossom, and a voice said, 'Don't hurt the blossom if you would see the fruit.' The interpretation: 'Be careful how you handle this revival, and the souls who have come into blessing. Grieve not the Spirit.' Criticism, or attributing to the flesh that which is of the Spirit, can hinder revival tremendously; let us not be guilty of either. Rather let us praise, worship, and adore our God and the Lamb, who looked upon us in our need and sent us 'times of refreshing' from His presence.

"Is the Revival spreading? Requests came from a neighbouring Mission for revival teams to be sent to two of their stations. They were sent, and God visited them in like manner as He visited us. Now a request has come for a team for another of their stations. We are convinced that wherever there is a genuine desire for revival and a willingness to accept what God sends, without any heart reservations, God will not pass them by. Let us humbly, by prayer and heart searching, seek God's face continually and be ready to pay the price for revival. Those of us who have experienced revival cannot praise God enough. He is the One who sent it, and He is the One who will maintain and cause it to spread. To Him be the Glory. Hallelujah!"

All glory to God, that a work has been wrought in our day in Congo which has the marks of eternity upon it, and which has changed and will change the face of His Church in Central Africa. How glorious to think that the exact centre of the once-dark continent has now been visited not only by the Word of the Gospel, but also by the accompaniment of the Holy Ghost sent down from heaven – which things the angels desire to look into. May it stimulate many of us to open the doors of our hearts and ministry wide to this same Blessed Visitor from on high.

WEC International has around 1800 workers drawn from over 40 countries in nearly 70 countries of the world. From its beginnings in the Congo in 1913 it has grown to work in many parts of the world. Evangelical and inter-denominational in outlook, WEC's ethos is based on Four Pillars of Faith, Sacrifice, Holiness, and Fellowship. WEC's commission is to bring the gospel of our Lord Jesus Christ to the remaining unevangelised peoples of the world with utmost urgency, to demonstrate the compassion of Christ to a needy world, to plant churches and lead them to spiritual maturity, and to inspire, mobilise and train for cross-cultural mission.

To help us achieve that, we have 16 Sending Bases scattered throughout the world which recruit, screen, send and help support workers. We also train missionary workers at six training institutes around the world.

WEC workers are involved in almost every type of direct outreach and support ministry related to the fulfilment of these aims. WEC's ministries range from the International Research Office that produces the prayer handbook *Operation World*, through the planting and establishment of churches, to the enabling of national missionary sending agencies in mature WEC fields.

Our Lifestyle

- We fervently desire to see Christ formed in us so that we live holy lives.
- In dependence on the Holy Spirit we determine to obey our Lord whatever the cost.
- We trust God completely to meet every need and challenge we face in His service.
- We are committed to oneness, fellowship and the care of our whole missionary family.

Our Convictions:

- We are convinced that prayer is a priority.
- We uphold biblical truth and standards.
- We affirm our love for Christ's Church, and endeavour to work in fellowship with local and national churches, and with other Christian agencies.
- We accept each other irrespective of gender, ethnic background or church affiliation.
- We desire to work in multi-national teams and are committed to effective international cooperation.
- We recognise the importance of research and responding to God's directions for advance.
- We believe in full participation and oneness in decision making.
- We value servant leaders who wait on God for vision and direction.
- We promote local and innovative strategies through decentralised decision making.
- We make no appeals for funds.

"If Jesus Christ be God and died for me, no sacrifice can be too great for me to make for Him."
C T Studd